Texas Hold'em
Fish 'n' Chips

A Beginners Guide

By
Jim Hodges

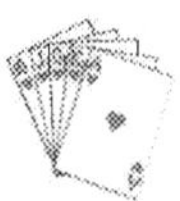

Order this book online at www.trafford.com
or email orders@trafford.com

Most Trafford titles are also available at major online book retailers.

Editors - Vicky Gillam, Ken Heslop

Printed in the United States of America.

ISBN: 978-1-4669-5713-8 (sc)
ISBN: 978-1-4669-5714-5 (e)

Library of Congress Control Number: 2012916941

Trafford rev. 12/13/2012

www.trafford.com

North America & international
toll-free: 1 888 232 4444 (USA & Canada)
phone: 250 383 6864 • fax: 812 355 4082

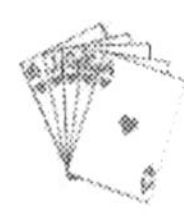

To Ken

My friend and poker partner
with whom many days and nights have been spent
playing, discussing, debating and dreaming.

You have inspired, motivated and kept me honest
while keeping the game fun.

You have always kept a smile on my face.

Thank you

TEXAS HOLD'EM

Fish 'n' Chips - A Beginners Guide

Table of Contents

INTRODUCTION 1

FOREWARD 3

GETTING STARTED 7

LESSON 1 - HAVE FUN!! 17

LESSON 2 - THE HANDS 19

ELEMENT 1: TERMS TO GET US STARTED 21
ELEMENT 2: STANDARD POKER HANDS 22
2.1 Royal Flush 23
2.2 Straight Flush 24
2.3 Four of a Kind (Quads) 25
2.4 Full House – (Full Boat) 26
2.5 Flush 28
2.6 Straight (Wheel) 30
2.7 Three of a Kind (Trips or Set) 31
2.8 Two Pair 33
2.9 One Pair 34
2.10 High Card 36

LESSON 3 - HAND EXAMPLES 38

LESSON 4 - HOW TO PLAY 64

ELEMENT 1: TERMS TO GET US STARTED 66
ELEMENT 2: PLAYING THE GAME 68
Stage 1 - Blinds Posted 69
Stage 2 - Hole Cards Dealt 70
Stage 3 - First Round of Betting 70

Stage 4 - The Flop 72
Stage 5 - Second Round of Betting 73
Stage 6 - The Turn 74
Stage 7 - Third Round of Betting 74
Stage 8 - The River 76
Stage 9 - Final Round of Betting 76
Element 3: The Rules & Etiquette 78
3.1 Rules 78
3.2 Etiquette 80

LESSON 5 - LET'S REVIEW 83

Element 1: Multiple Choice Quiz 84
Element 2: Short Answer Questions 86
Element 3: Crossword 88

LESSON 6 - THREE IMPORTANT FACTORS 91

Element 1: Terms to Get Us Started 93
Element 2: Cards You Possess 94
2.1 169 Possibilities 94
2.2 Top 10 Best Hands 95
2.3 The Worst Starting Hands 97
2.4 Hands and Ranks 100
2.5 Common Hand Names 103
2.6 Common Hole Card Names 104
Element 3: Chip Stack 105
Element 4: Table Position 108
Element 5: Starting Hands to Play 112

LESSON 7 - GAME MANAGEMENT 115

Element 1: Bankroll Management 116
1.1 Cash Game Bankroll 120
1.2 Tournament Bankroll 121
Element 2: Tracking Results 124

LESSON 8 - HOME GAMES & PRACTICE EXERCISES.............134

ELEMENT 1: TERMS TO GET US STARTED 135
ELEMENT 2: ON-LINE GAMES..136
ELEMENT 3: HOME GAMES 143
3.1 Establishing a Home Game...143
3.2 Home Game Structure 156

LESSON 9 - THE “PEA” PRINCIPLE 163

ELEMENT 1: PERSEVERANCE..165
ELEMENT 2: EDUCATION 169
ELEMENT 3: ASSOCIATION...173

LESSON 10 - A LITTLE MORE REVIEW 177

ELEMENT 1: MULTIPLE CHOICE QUIZ 178
ELEMENT 2: SHORT ANSWER QUESTIONS 181
ELEMENT 3: TRUE OR FALSE 183

LESSON 11 - LEARNING OUR LANGUAGE 185

ELEMENT 1: STUDYING THE LANGUAGE A - J..........................186
ELEMENT 2: CROSSWORD CHALLENGE A – J..........................195
ELEMENT 3: STUDYING THE LANGUAGE K – Z........................198
ELEMENT 4: CROSSWORD CHALLENGE K - Z 205

LESSON 12 - WHERE TO GO FROM HERE?.............................208

ELEMENT 1: FOLLOWING THE “PEA” 209
ELEMENT 2: PLAY, PLAY, PLAY..216
ELEMENT 3: MY TOP TEN TIPS 217

FISH ‘N’ CHIPS - ANSWER GUIDE...222

ACKNOWLEDGEMENTS...235

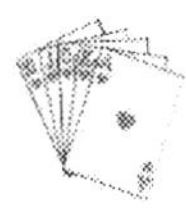

INTRODUCTION

I was born in England in 1965 however, due to work opportunities offered to my father, I spent most of my childhood growing up on the South Island of New Zealand. At the age of 14 my parents divorced and I moved to Australia with my mother and brother.

In 1982, the day before my 17th birthday, I joined the Royal Australian Navy (R.A.N.) as an electrical apprentice and began a career which would span the next 23 years. It was during these years that I truly developed a love for cards and a game we referred to as "Uckers" (a traditional R.A.N. board game that is a cross between Parcheesi and Ludo). Although I played several card games regularly, only one was really considered to be the true Navy game – "500", and it was at this game I excelled.

I retired from the R.A.N. in January 2006 and took up a position in a small town called Airlie Beach in North Queensland, Australia better known for its beautiful islands, national parks and tourist hot spots. It was here that I began my second career as a teacher of Computing, Business Administration and Management courses at the local technical college. A life spent in the Defence Force doesn't always allow the time and the freedom to pursue hobbies and interests or get involved in community groups for a great length of time, and so once settled I took up the interests that had eluded me for so many years. A little fishing, some boating and the opportunity to spend quality time with my family and friends without fear of deployment.

My passion for Texas Hold'em Poker began in November 2007 while watching the late night games on satellite TV and being entertained by the likes of Joe Hachem, Gus Hansen, Phil Ivey, Daniel Negreanu and Chris Ferguson to name but a few. I had never really considered poker as a possible hobby, let alone an obsession, and yet the more I watched the more I found myself drawn into the world of poker, its stars and the minor soap dramas which seemed to accompany many of the championship matches.

It was actually during one of those late nights watching yet another drama unfold in a previous World Series match that an advertisement appeared for "PokerStars" and my wife suggested that I have a look at the site and perhaps join. At this stage I had only a basic grasp of Texas Hold'em rules, strategy and game play but decided that this might be fun. The next day I logged onto the internet and joined the site.

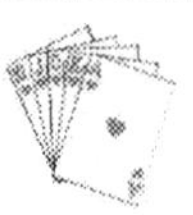

I began playing and found myself increasingly getting drawn deeper and deeper into the world of Texas Hold'em. I quickly realised that this newfound passion was going to require a serious amount of time and energy dedicated to grasping the basic fundamentals, let alone advanced strategies.

So with the vigour and determination that tends to consume me when I get involved in a new project, I took the big dive into the world of poker with the attitude that if I am going to do this I am going to do it to the best of my ability. To achieve my goals I would have to play, read, watch and absorb as much poker as I could comfortably manage. I certainly did not want poker to become all consuming however, I believe that to be successful in anything we must follow what I refer to as the PEA principle – Perseverance, Education & Association. I will discuss this principle in more detail later in the book.

I hear another comment from the peanut gallery of life where any uninformed ignoramus is entitled to an opinion and the right to voice it - "Oh, poker is all about luck", "just another coin toss", "you really don't require any special skills to win". The knot tightens in my stomach and my heart begins to race as the feeling of blood boiling begins to consume me. I know that my frustration is born of defects in my own character - impatience and intolerance. Both areas I know I need to work on regularly, but give me a break!

The players I have grown to admire and respect in this most challenging of games do not and have not continued to succeed and excel because they are grouped among the luckiest people on this planet. In truth, they are extremely skilled, patient, determined and driven individuals who in most cases have spent years, even decades, refining and honing their art. Sure, luck plays a small part and anybody with any understanding of the game would not deny this, but in the immortal words of Thomas Jefferson:-

"I'm a great believer in luck, and I find the harder I work, the more I have of it."

For now though, please sit back and enjoy what I hope is a wonderful introduction to the word of Texas Hold'em.

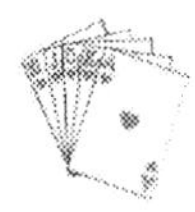

FOREWARD

Fish

To be called a fish in the realms of poker is to be told that you are unskilled, unworthy, plain hopeless or that you have played a hand carelessly, possibly risking money or chips on a long shot.

There is also a phrase among poker players, "Don't tap on the aquarium." It means don't upset the bad players because they may leave and take your future winnings / earnings with them.

You may also hear the term "Donkey", this also has a similar meaning. To be called a fish or a donkey is about as high an insult as you can get when playing poker.

One point I will make on the subject of fish. You are going to come across a wide variety of players from all walks of life and with all kinds of attitude, some great, some not so great. Don't get discouraged if you come across the occasional player who cannot help being rude, crude or obnoxious. Just remember, it is they who have the issue and you are there to learn – ignore them and move on.

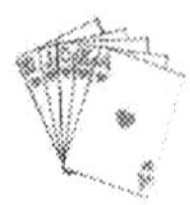

Chips

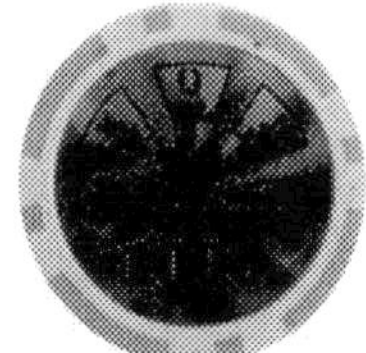

The game of poker originated in the middle of the 1800's and was predominantly played on the river boats, bars and in saloons of the mid-west in America. Gold dust, nuggets and coins were originally used to bet however this method proved to be inefficient and a substitute for money was soon introduced - The "Chip".

The guy who invented poker was bright,
but the guy who invented the chip was a genius.

Julius "Big Julie" Weintraub
(Ex-professional basketball player and gambler)

The original chips used by gambling establishments were made from ivory, bone, wood and even paper in some cases. The trouble with these chips was that they were easily copied and so began many years of innovation, trials and changes in an effort to eliminate this problem.

The humble chip really came of age in the 1940's with the introduction of plastic. For the first time, cheap and durable chips were available to the masses and as such the popularity of poker rose. Today a standard chip is 39 millimetres in diameter with a weight ranging from 8.5 grams to 20.5 grams. It is made from composite materials and for those used in casinos they often have microchips inserted to prevent forgery.

It is a Chinese proverb that states:

"Tell me and I'll forget;
Show me and I may remember;
Involve me and I'll understand."

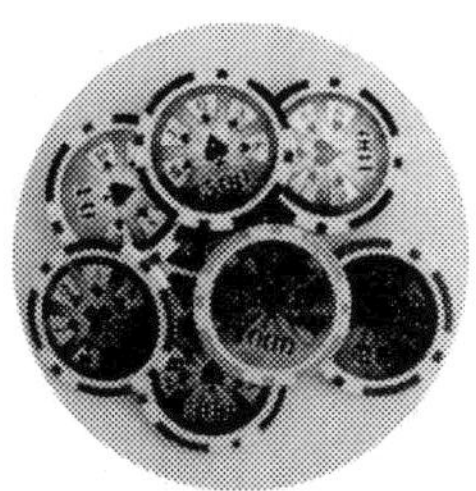

PLEASE – Get Involved!

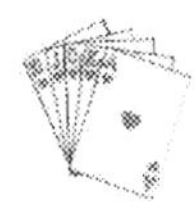

GETTING STARTED

"The spirit, the will to win, and the will to excel are the things that endure. These qualities are so much more important than the events that occur."

Vincent Lombardi
(American Football coach)

Speaking for myself, the last four years have proven to be an enormous learning curve, one that has been challenging and extremely enjoyable. Through the hundreds of on-line tournaments, cash games, home games, bar games, books and television shows I have learned several very big lessons, lessons which have allowed me to progress from complete poker novice to a poker player who now plays with a regular profit margin.

It is my wish to involve you in the process that I have used, refined and continue to build on in order to learn how to play this exciting game to the best of my ability. This is not simply a book talking about experiences nor is it a set of basic instructions with the empty promise of riches at the end of a rainbow. This book is meant to be used as a guide and a tool, one developed over four years of playing, reading, studying and watching the game I have grown to love. It has been drawn together with the sole purpose of taking you through a step-by-step process I have used in order to improve and make my game successful.

I must mention at this stage, my definition of success. I love poker, the characters involved, the excitement, the thrill of the chase and I love the way the game has given me another common interest with my wife. Poker has brought a small group of our friends together whose hectic lives would otherwise have kept distance between us. Instead, we now make time every three weeks to come together and not only play, but share small moments with each other and then get together on-line each Sunday night, simply do battle and have a laugh. Success to me is about being truly happy in life and the pursuits you undertake. I love every aspect of the game. Could I one day handle playing for a living? I would like to think so. Could I one day be making more money than I am today in my job? I can but chase that dream. Today I am happy in my progress and content at my level. Today I am successful.

If it is your wish to become successful in Texas Hold'em I suggest you begin by reading this book, cover to cover. Do not do any of the exercises, do not follow any of the instructions, simply read the book and get a feel for where this journey is about to take you. Just like in the days when we sat for an exam and the first written instruction was, "please read all of this paper before you begin" - I know most of us didn't. In this case, please do. Once you have done so I would suggest that you then go back to the start and begin doing to exercises.

Throughout this book you are going to be asked to perform certain tasks before you proceed to the next section or chapter. Please have a go and do your best. Quite simply, in coming to the point where I could lay down a clear path for you to follow, I had to make a lot of mistakes and waste a substantial amount of time and money. This is all part of the process of learning and poker. I do not want you to make the same mistakes I made. That is not to say that you are not going to make mistakes along the way. In fact I am a firm believer that most of our "big" lessons in life are learnt from making mistakes or doing things incorrectly.

I also do not want you to throw a whole lot of money away playing games that are not profitable. By profitable I am also talking about games that teach you skills without necessarily making a lot of money to begin with. I am suggesting that you reduce the amount of time you spend pursuing foolish errands so that you are better able to bring your game to a profitable stage sooner. In writing this book and working my game until it became profitable, I read approximately 25 books and waded through countless articles and magazine editorials. In addition to the hundreds of hours spent watching any tournament I could find on television, I also got involved in as many local live tournaments as I could manage as well as starting and running a poker club for a group of about 15 friends.

First and foremost you must ask yourself a simple question.

"What do I want to achieve playing poker?"

That may seem like a very basic question, with what may seem to be a very basic answer – I want to win and make money! One of the biggest lessons I have learned in life is that if your primary motivation for doing something is simply to make money then simply – you won't! Your primary motivation should be based upon something far deeper. I think the same can be said for poker. Over the past four years I have become very

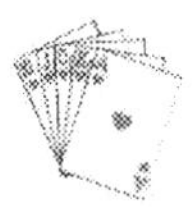

passionate about poker and it is for the following reasons (in order of importance) I love to play and be involved:-

1. Poker has provided my wife and I with another common interest;
2. Poker has brought a group of our friends closer together;
3. I love competition and the challenge associated with pursuing improvement;
4. I love to win ☺;
5. I love the rush and the adrenaline associated with playing;
6. I love to make money.

When I first had the thought that I wanted to better my game, write this book and maybe help others realise a dream, I had a program in mind whereby I would be professional poker player in four years. Not an unrealistic goal in my mind, but nonetheless a goal that came from a person who really still had no idea about how to play the game – such arrogance? Perhaps so!

Today my motives for playing are still as stated above. I hope to wake up one day and realise that I am making more money playing poker than I am in my day job and it will be that realisation which will take me on another journey. For the moment though, I understand that effort and commitment are going to be required to further improve my game and take it to new levels

I imagine your reasons for playing poker are different to mine but at the end of the day it is important that we ask ourselves several questions with regard to playing the game. Use the following section to note your thoughts.

Why are you here? *(Use my reasons provided as a guide)*

What past experiences have you had playing poker? *(Have you ever played or excelled in other games or competitions?)*

What level do you want to achieve? *(Do you want to be a break even player or would you like to make a living from the game?)*

What abilities do you possess and what are you good at? (*Here is an opportunity to look at your own strengths and weaknesses.)*

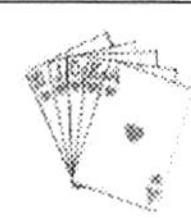

What type of skills do you need to develop? *(Eg: you may want to learn about body language in order to read players better.)*

What are you willing to do to achieve your goals? What type of commitments are you willing to make. (*Eg: Reading a book a week, playing 10 hours a week, etc.)*

What resources will you need? (*Eg: How much money can you afford to invest in your training? Will you require software or coaching?)*

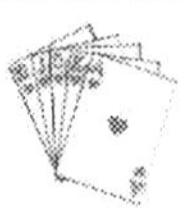

What are the barriers to your progress? (*Eg: work related issues, family or financial.)*

What are going to be your measures of success? (*Eg: I would like to finish this year $1,000 in front. I would like to have a good home group established.)*

Are there any other considerations you think may impact on your commitment to poker?

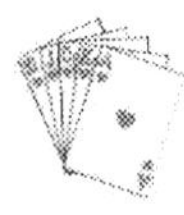

You may find over time that your reasons for playing change. Use your responses as a means to reflect on where your game has taken you. Do you still play for the same motivation or has it changed?

Now that you have identified the reasons behind your desire to play, it is also important to identify what you hope to achieve. Once you have identified what you want to achieve it is time to set some goals. Another great life lesson for me is the understanding that goal setting is extremely important in all aspects of our lives. Why is goal setting in relation to poker important for you?

"Goals determine what you're going to be."
- Julius Erving
(Professional basketball player)

To begin to understand goal setting you must learn a couple of basic concepts as well as be willing to exercise some discipline in relation to your goals. I have included one of the most common tools used to help establish viable goals - SMART. The acronym spells out criteria for goals that are:

Specific

Measurable

Achievable

Relevant

Time-based

SMART goals provide you with the means of incorporating discipline in your planning or training process. Application of this approach will enable you to focus on the future and establish goals that will create a roadmap for success. Goals that meet these standards will provide greater opportunities for accomplishment than those that are stated in a vague, general or hopeful manner, or not stated at all.

Defining and Stating a SMART Goal

A *Specific* goal is stated in well-defined, specific terms (e.g. increase, establish, reduce) that focus on desired future results and leave no doubt as to what is to be achieved.

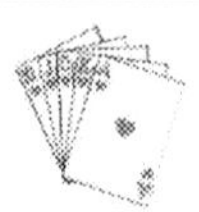

A *Measurable* goal statement includes numeric and/or descriptive terms that will allow you to understand with certainty that the defined results have been accomplished.

An *Achievable* goal is one that is attainable but still presents a realistic challenge. This is important because quite often individuals "set themselves up for failure" by establishing a bar that cannot be overcome, the result being that they quit setting goals because it has become too difficult.

A *Relevant* goal is meaningful and will make a difference if accomplished. The goal needs to bring something positive to your life.

Goals need to be *Time-based* and require beginning and ending dates. It is pointless establishing a goal that does not have limitations on time because without these parameters goals become vague and unattainable. A timetable instils a sense of urgency that can provide motivation and keep moving us forward.

I understand that if you are here to learn how to play poker and have very limited experience in the game then setting poker goals may seem a little foreign. Once again, feel free to complete this section after you have played a few games and got a feel for the type of goals you may wish to set.

Below is an example of a SMART goal. Complete the table following and identify the poker goal that you consider to be the most relevant.

Specific: - My specific goal is to increase my bankroll from $1000 to $2200 in a 12 month period.

Measurable: - I will measure my progress by checking my bankroll and ensure it is increasing by $100 per month

Attainable: - I will play three 25c/50c cash games and one $20 nine-man tournament per week.

Realistic: - Wednesdays, Fridays and Saturdays are the only days I can set aside for poker and only from midday to 9.00pm each day.

Timely: - I will achieve my goal in twelve months however, it will be reviewed and readjusted if required in six months.

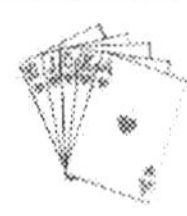

MY POKER GOAL

Specific:	
Measurable:	
Attainable:	
Realistic:	
Timely:	

Now we understand the reasons that we are here and we have set a few goals. It is time to jump into the game and begin learning the fundamentals of poker.

Good Luck!!

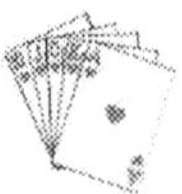

Research Question 1

Who currently has the most
World Series of Poker (WSOP) bracelets?

Try and find out the answers to the Research Questions from the multitude of websites dedicated to Texas Hold-em Poker that are out there on the internet.

[If you really want to find out the answers to the Research Questions now, they are contained on page 232.]

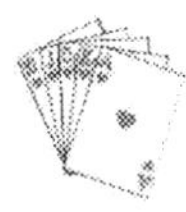

LESSON 1 – HAVE FUN!!

Don't take yourself or others too seriously but balance this with your desire to win.

My good friend Ken once told me a story which concluded with –

"You're not good enough to get mad,
just have fun and everything will fall into place".

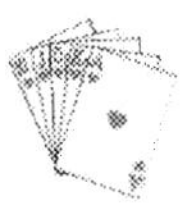

LESSON 2 - THE HANDS

" It is our attitude at the beginning of a difficult undertaking which, more than anything else, will determine its successful outcome. "

William James
(Considered the father of American psychology)

So here you are - on the verge of indulging an addiction, about to develop a passion or simply looking for another fun way to pass the time. Before you go rushing off to the nearest casino, bar or local home game, let's get a grasp of the basics.

No doubt you have seen a few games played locally, on line or on TV but this is not the time to get into anything higher stake than a little "play money". First things first – remember we are learning to walk here.

Texas Hold'em Poker is a relatively simple yet deceptively challenging game to learn to play and as you will soon discover an even harder game to master. (Can anyone say that they have truly mastered the game?) The most important first step in learning to play poker is to fully understand the rank structure or value of each hand in relation to the other hands. Being able to recognise both current and potential hands is vital, for without a firm grasp of this basic concept your poker playing career / hobby will never get off the ground.

It never ceases to amaze me how many people play poker without understanding this most basic of requirements. Does a flush beat a straight? Does two pair beat three of a kind? This is the equivalent of driving a car without knowing where the brake is and yet I still occasionally run into people who are not completely clear on which hands are stronger than others. (Having said that, once in a blue moon I have missed a hand, but I learnt a long time ago to keep those little absentminded mistakes to myself!). If you are not interested in being known as the local fish or donkey, then this is most definitely the first part of poker that you need to get a handle on.

I can tell you there is no worse feeling in poker than getting beaten in a hand where the person who has won either did not realise they had won because they didn't fully understand the hand ranks or they have simply kept chasing impossible odds only to go on and find victory. We must

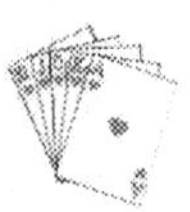

realise though that this also is part of poker. Instead of criticising, complaining, or falling into a major self-pity party we must pick ourselves up and spend time learning how to deal with those situations both mentally and emotionally. This is one of the main aspects of the game that I spent a lot of time working on.

Learning Outcomes

In this lesson we will be learning several new terms and phrases as well as taking a closer look at the hands of Texas Hold'em. By the conclusion of this lesson you should be able to identify all of the possible hands, their order of strength and also be familiar with all of the terminology used to this point.

Element 1: Terms to Get Us Started

Element 2: Standard Poker Hands

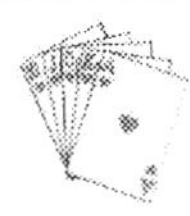

Element 1: Terms to Get Us Started

Board – The set of face up community cards. .

Community Cards – Cards dealt face-up in the centre of the table that can be used by all players in the action.

Full Boat – Full House.

Kicker – The kicker is used to determine a winner when hands are tied.

Over Card - A community card with a higher rank than any player's pocket pair.

Quads - Four of a Kind.

Split Pot – Usually the result of a tie where each player tied takes an equal share of the pot.

Straight (Wheel) – run of five cards in sequence.

Trips / Set – Three of a kind.

Did You Know –
A Pair of Aces (A-A) is known by several different terms. Bullets, pocket rockets or American Airlines?

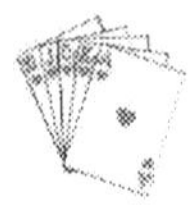

Element 2: Standard Poker Hands

The standard hands in Texas Hold 'em Poker ranked highest to lowest are:-

- 2.1 Royal Flush
- 2.2 Straight Flush
- 2.3 Four of a Kind (Quads)
- 2.4 Full House (Full Boat)
- 2.5 Flush
- 2.6 Straight (Wheel)
- 2.7 Three of a Kind (Trips or Set)
- 2.8 Two Pair
- 2.9 One Pair
- 2.10 High Card

The cards in poker are ranked from Ace to King with the Ace representing both the highest and lowest in value. In the case of a low end straight (A-2-3-4-5) the Ace is the lowest card. In every other case the Ace is considered the highest ranked card.

The suits do not differ in value and as such all suits are considered equal.

Following is a breakdown of the standard poker hands.

Did You Know –
A pair of Kings (K-K) is known by several different terms, Cowboys, Elvis Presley, and King Kong?

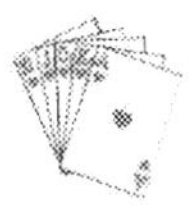

2.1 Royal Flush

The Ace-high Straight Flush is commonly referred to as a Royal Flush.

This hand is the Holy Grail of poker as it is extremely difficult to obtain and by virtue of that fact, the most powerful hand in poker. At the time of writing I have only ever been dealt two Royal Flush hands and have only ever seen two others played.

A Royal Flush consists of five cards in numerical sequence, all of the same suit, beginning with a 10 and finishing with the Ace, the highest valued card. This hand can only be obtained by one player (unless the hand appears on the table or board), and as such it requires all five cards to complete this hand.

Did you know -
A pair of Queens (Q-Q) is generally referred to as "Ladies"?

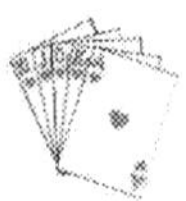

2.2 Straight Flush

The Straight Flush is also very difficult to obtain and is ranked as the second highest hand possible. A Straight Flush consists of five cards in numerical sequence, all of the same suit.

In the event that two players have a straight flush then the player with the highest card will win the pot.

Example

Community Cards

Opponents Cards

My Cards (Winner)

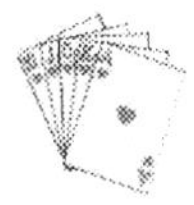

2.3 Four of a Kind (Quads)

Another very powerful hand and a beauty to behold when you do hit a hand of this calibre. The Four of a Kind consists of four cards of the same value.

If during play the Four of a Kind hand is shown in the community cards then the hand with the highest valued "kicker" wins.

Example

Community Cards

Opponents cards (King kicker)

My Cards (Ace kicker)

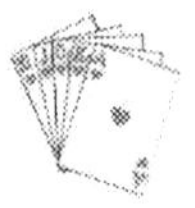

2.4 Full House – (Full Boat)

A Full House remains a powerful hand at number four on the rankings scale and is the type of hand that you will see with a little more regularity. It consists of a three of a kind and a pair.

The important thing to remember is that if more than one player has a full house then the strongest hand is determined firstly by the value of the three of a kind with the highest one winning.

However, if both players have the same three of a kind then, the win will be awarded to the player who holds the highest valued pair. In the example below, the pair of Kings beats the pair of 10's.

Example 1

Community Cards

Opponents Cards

My Cards (Winner)

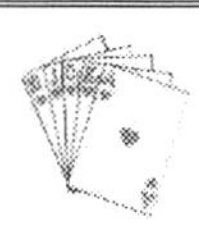

It is also possible that both players have the same valued hand in which case it is a split pot and the winnings divided evenly. I have experienced several games where a little confusion has arisen over these particular scenarios, because of the "kicker".

Example 2

Community Cards

Opponents Cards

My Cards

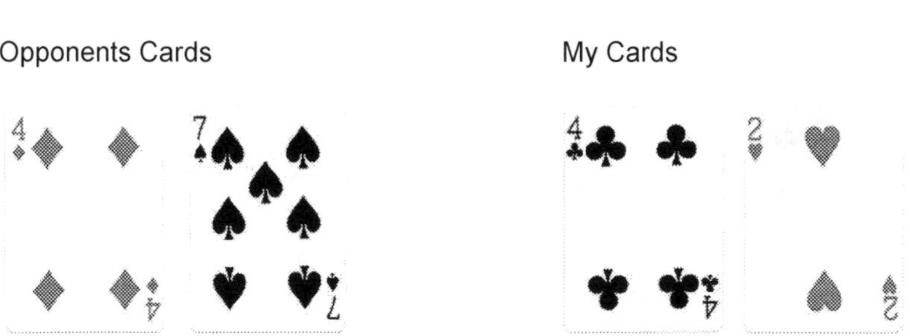

As five cards are required to complete a full house the kicker will not come into play. Therefore this will be a split pot.

Did You Know -
A-Q is known as Little Slick, Big Chick, or Mrs. Slick?

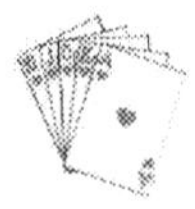

2.5 Flush

The Flush consists of five cards of the same suit while the strength of the flush is determined by the highest valued card in the hand.

Example 1

Community Cards

Opponents Cards

My Cards (Winner)

In Example 1 we see an "Ace high" flush of the community cards as they have been dealt. Both players have made a flush - however both players also hold a spade. As the hand requires the five highest spades, I win the hand as I hold the Queen.

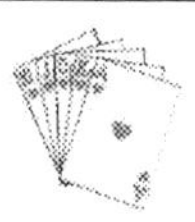

Example 2

Community Cards

Opponents Cards

My Cards (Winner)

In Example 2 we see that we have been dealt three cards to a spade flush giving both players a flush. My opponent has a Jack high flush because of the community Jack and I have a Queen high flush because of the card I hold, giving me the win.

Did You Know -
K-Q suited is known as a royal marriage while K-Q unsuited is referred to as a mixed marriage?

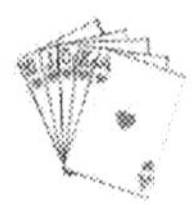

2.6 Straight (Wheel)

Straights are far more common than the previous hands and occur with quite a bit of frequency. They are still a relatively powerful hand and can often come from the most unlikely of hands.

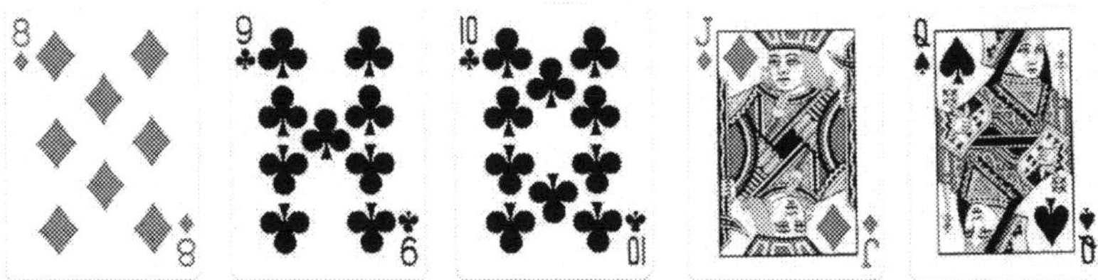

Straights are made up of five cards in numerical sequence with 10-J-Q-K-A being the highest and A-2-3-4-5 being the lowest. These hands are not suited, otherwise it would be a Straight Flush.

Example 1

Community Cards

Opponents Cards

My Cards (Winner)

In Example 1 we can see that both players have made a straight. My opponent is holding the low straight 8-9-10-J-Q while I have made a high straight with 10-J-Q-K-A.

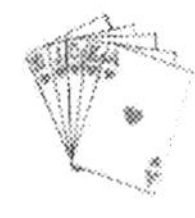

2.7 Three of a Kind (Trips or Set)

Quite self-explanatory, the three of a kind hand is made up of three cards of the same numerical value plus two kickers.

As the three of a kind only makes up 3/5 of our hand, it becomes extremely important that we pay attention to the other two cards (kickers) that are involved. (Don't forget, if we have a pair to go with this hand then we would have a Full House.)

Example 1

Community Cards

Opponents Cards

My Cards (Winner)

As can be seen in Example 1 each player has got Trip 3's, however the next highest card is my King and so therefore I would win the hand.

Example 2

Community Cards

Opponents Cards

My Cards (Winner)

In Example 2 each player has got Trip 7's and an Ace kicker but the next highest card is my Queen so I would win the hand.

Did You Know -
A-K is commonly known as "Big Slick" however it also is known by other names such as Anna Kournikova (looks good but rarely wins), and Machine Gun (AK-47)?

2.8 Two Pair

In Texas Hold'em, two pair is statistically the hand which wins the most hands. Once again the kicker comes into play if both players hold two pair of equal value.

In the example we see that both players have made a pair with their Queen and the community Queen. In addition, the board has a pair of 3's giving each player two pair. Because the next highest card is my Jack I then win the hand.

Example 1

Community Cards

Opponents Cards

My Cards (Winner)

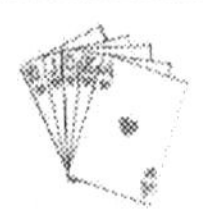

2.9 One Pair

A hand with One Pair is very common and as such should be played cautiously.

In Example 1 each player has got a pair of Aces, but the next highest card is my King kicker so I would win the hand.

Example 1

Community Cards

Opponents Cards

My Cards (Winner)

Did You Know -
A-J is referred to as Blackjack, Ajax or Jackass?

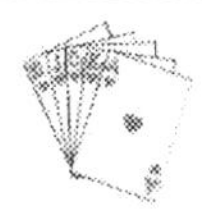

Example 2

Community Cards

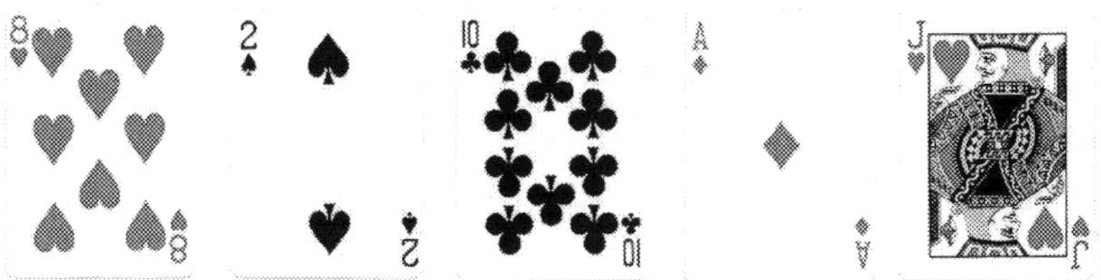

Opponents Cards

My Cards (Winner)

In Example 2 my opponent has hit a pair however so have I and my pair is higher so therefore I win the hand. These types of situations are common and as such we need to be aware of over cards.

Did You Know -
A pair of Jacks (J-J) is known as Fishhooks, Hooks, Jokers, or Johnnies

There is a saying in among Texas Hold'em players. "There are only three ways to play a pair of Jacks - check, raise or fold; and they are all wrong."

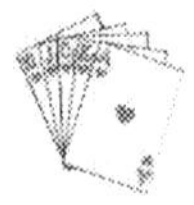

2.10 High Card

If a hand does not fit into any of the other hand categories then the strength of the hand is determined by the highest card that each players hold. Given that five cards are required to make a hand, if two players have the same High Card then we go to the next highest card and so on and so forth until a winner is decided.

Example 1

Community Cards

Opponents Cards (Winner)

My Cards

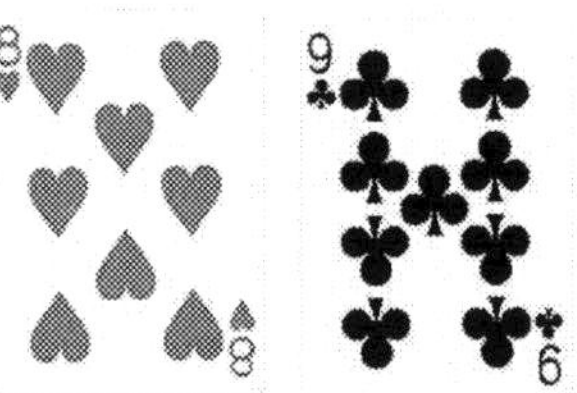

In this example, neither player has "hit" their hand. In that case, we must see which player has the highest card.

Both players share the Ace and King and the next highest card is my opponent's Jack and as such wins the hand.

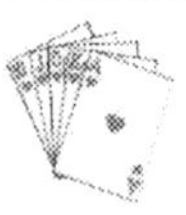

This brings us to the end of Lesson 2 and I hope that you have now come away with a clearer understanding of the hand ranks and structures.

If you are not completely sure please review this lesson.

Fear not - for in Lesson 3 we will be running through some practice examples and putting your hand recognition to the test.

Research Question 2

Who are the only two people to have ever won the WSOP Main Event three times?

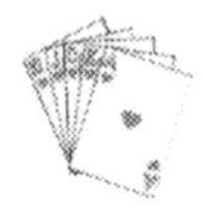

LESSON 3 - HAND EXAMPLES

"To give yourself the best possible chance of playing to your potential, you must prepare for every eventuality. That means practice."

Severiano Ballesteros
(Professional golfer)

Learning Outcomes

In the following group of fifteen exercises view the hands presented then make a determination as to which hand you believe would win that round. I have based these hands on the types of hands that can occasionally cause concern or confusion.

KEY

Use the key below to identify each of the hands in the space provided then at the bottom of the page record the player that you feel would have won that round and the hand they received.

Hand	Key
High Card	HC
Pair	Pr
Two Pair	2P
Three of a Kind	3oK
Straight	Str
Flush	Fsh
Four of a Kind	4oK
Straight Flush	SFsh
Royal Flush	RFs

Remember: We are making the best 'five' card hand out of a total of seven cards and so the community cards are as the name suggests, belonging to everyone playing.

All answers can be found the Fish 'n' Chips Answer Guide on page 222.

Good Luck and have fun!!

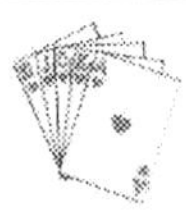

EXERCISE 1

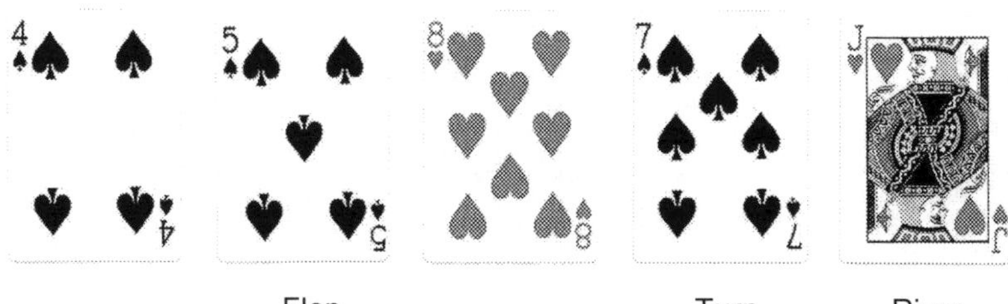

Flop Turn River

Player 1 ______________ Player 2 ______________

Player 3 ______________ Player 4 ______________

Which Player has the best hand and why?

____

EXERCISE 2

Flop Turn River

Player 1 ______________

Player 2 ______________

Player 3 ______________

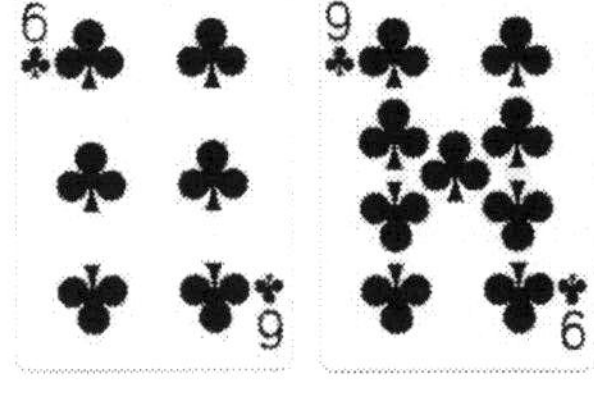

Player 4 ______________

Which Player has the best hand and why?

____

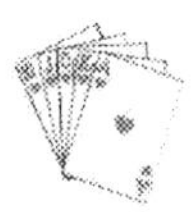

EXERCISE 3

Flop Turn River

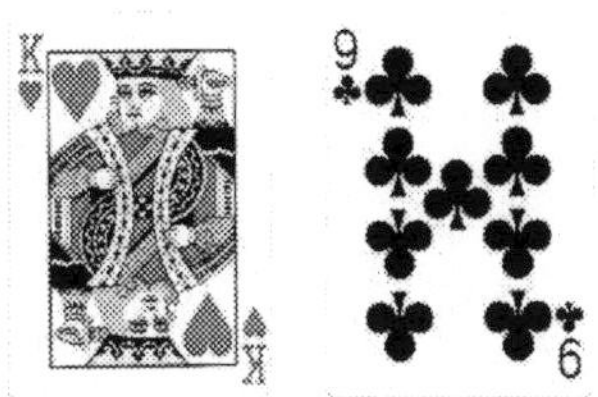

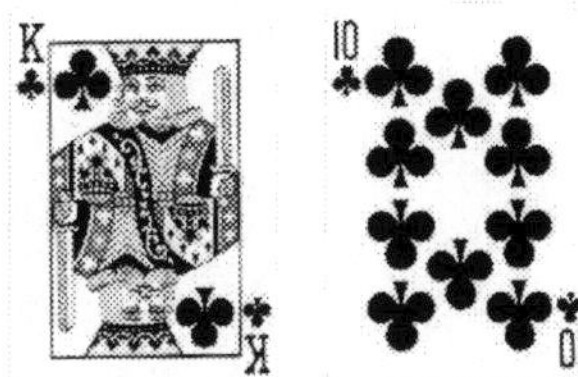

Player 1 ______________ Player 2 ______________

Player 3 ______________ Player 4 ______________

Which Player has the best hand and why?

____

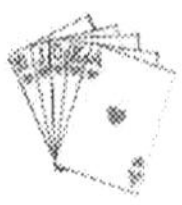

EXERCISE 4

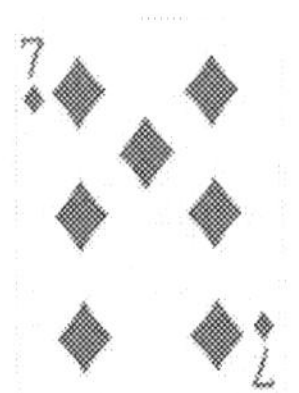

Flop Turn River

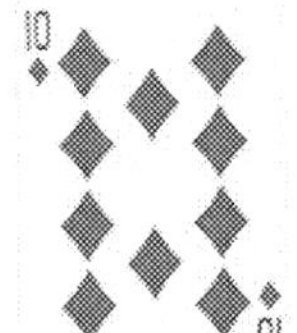

Player 1 ______________ Player 2 ______________

Player 3 ______________ Player 4 ______________

Which Player has the best hand and why?

____

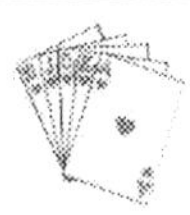

EXERCISE 5

Flop Turn River

Player 1 _______________ Player 2 _______________

Player 3 _______________ Player 4 _______________

Which Player has the best hand and why?

____

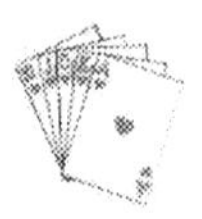

EXERCISE 6

Flop Turn River

Player 1 ______________

Player 2 

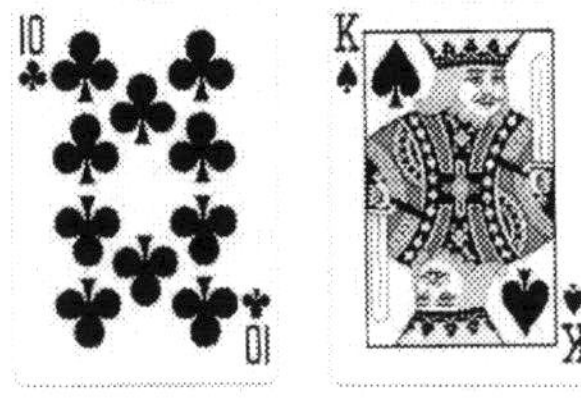

Player 3 ______________

Player 4 ______________

Which Player has the best hand and why?

____

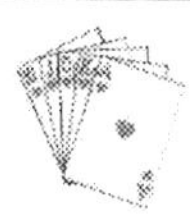

EXERCISE 7

Flop Turn River

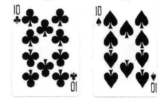

Player 1 ______________ Player 2 ______________

Player 3 ______________ Player 4 ______________

Which Player has the best hand and why?

____

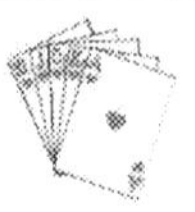

EXERCISE 8

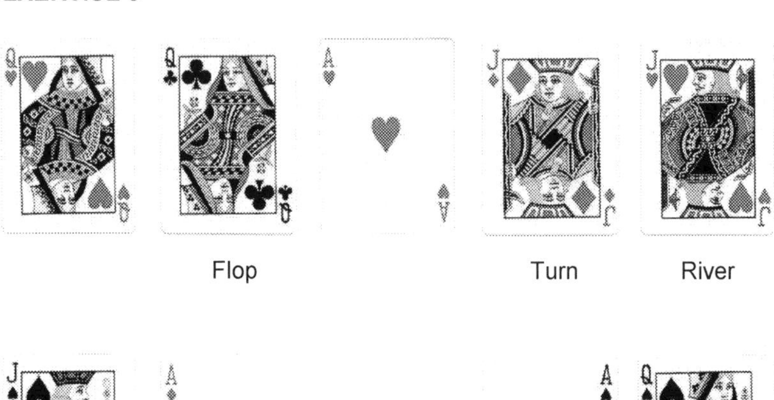

Flop Turn River

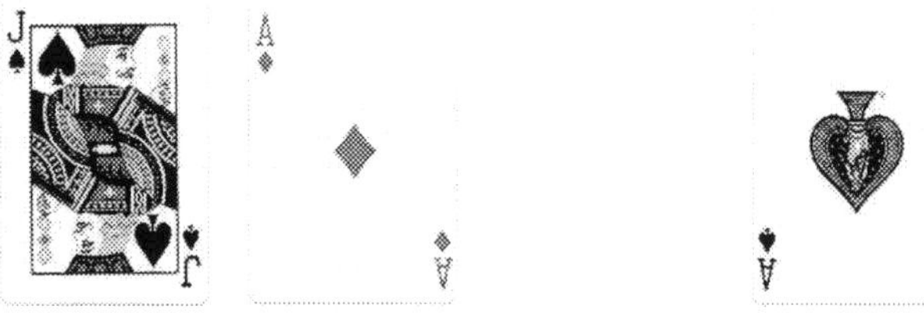

Player 1 ______________ Player 2 ______________

Player 3 ______________ Player 4 ______________

Which Player has the best hand and why?

____

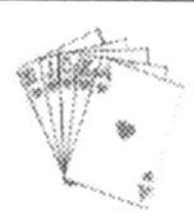

EXERCISE 9

Flop Turn River

Player 1 _______________

Player 2 _______________

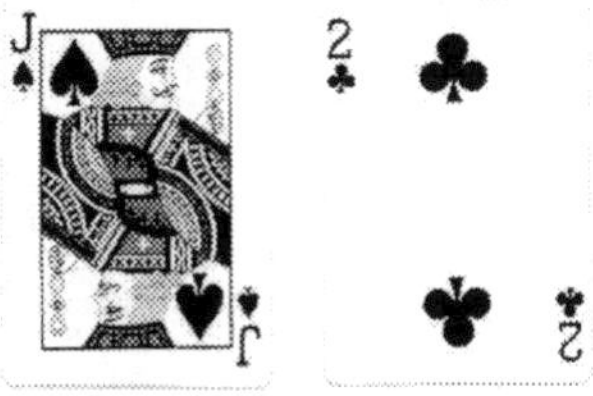

Player 3 _______________

Player 4 _______________

Which Player has the best hand and why?

____

EXERCISE 10

Flop Turn River

Player 1 ______________

Player 2 ______________

Player 3 ______________

Player 4 ______________

Which Player has the best hand and why?

____

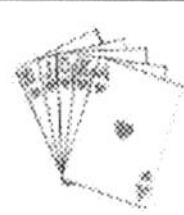

EXERCISE 11

Flop Turn River

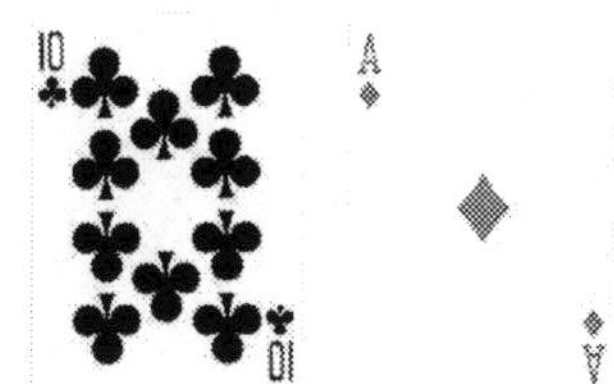

Player 1 ______________ Player 2 ______________

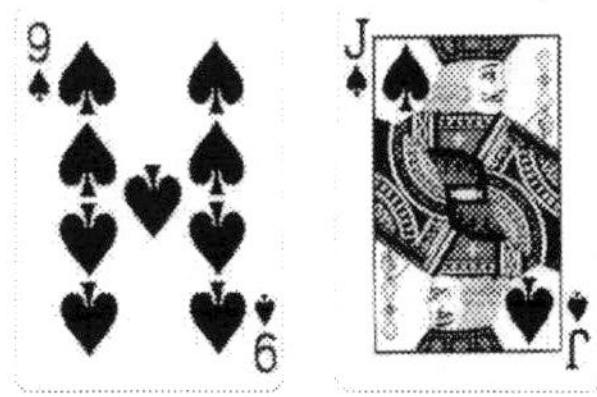

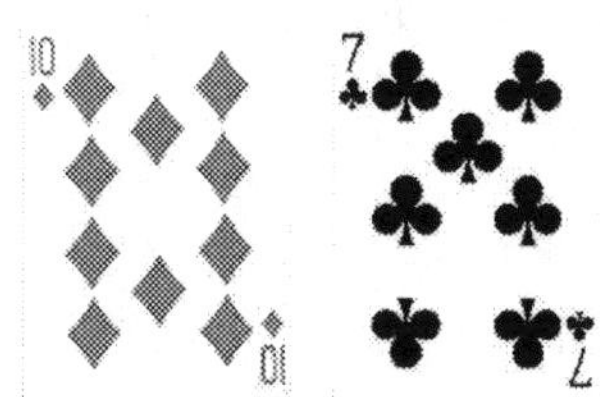

Player 3 ______________ Player 4 ______________

Which Player has the best hand and why?

____

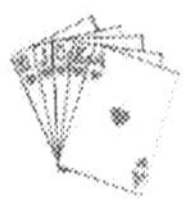

EXERCISE 12

Flop Turn River

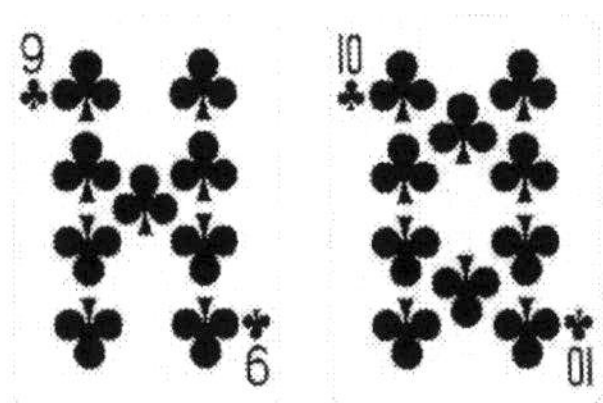

Player 1 ______________ Player 2 ______________

Player 3 ______________ Player 4 ______________

Which Player has the best hand and why?

____

EXERCISE 13

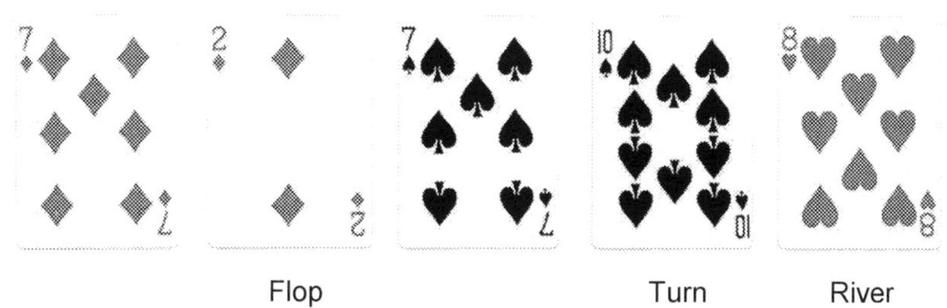

Flop Turn River

Player 1 ______________

Player 2 ______________

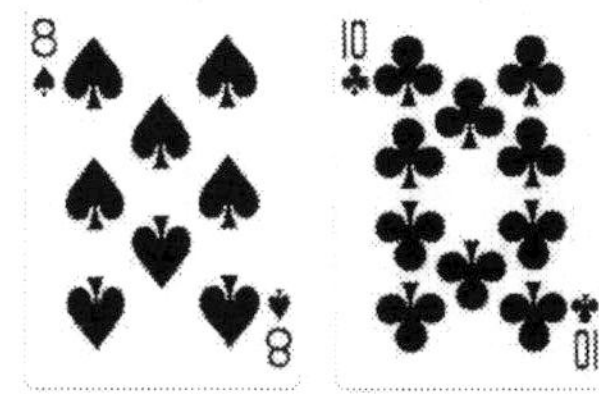

Player 3 ______________

Player 4 ______________

Which Player has the best hand and why?

____

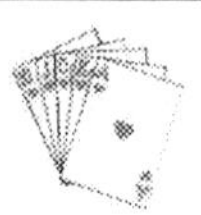

EXERCISE 14

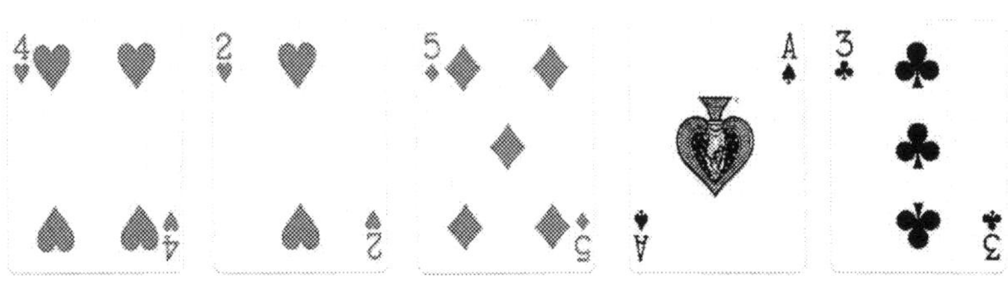

Flop Turn River

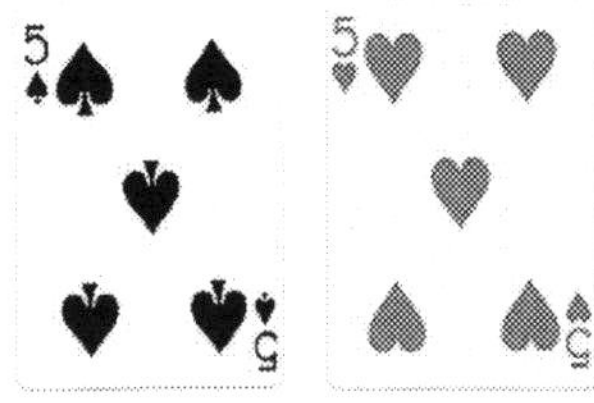

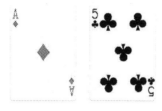

Player 1 ______________ Player 2 ______________

Player 3 ______________ Player 4 ______________

Which Player has the best hand and why?

____

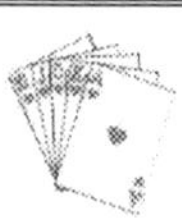

EXERCISE 15

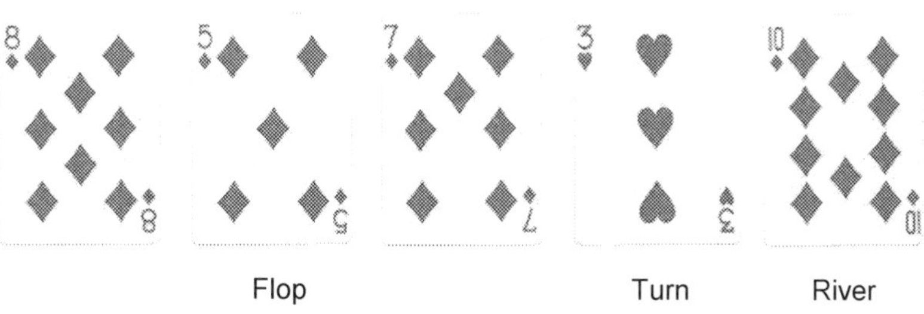

Flop Turn River

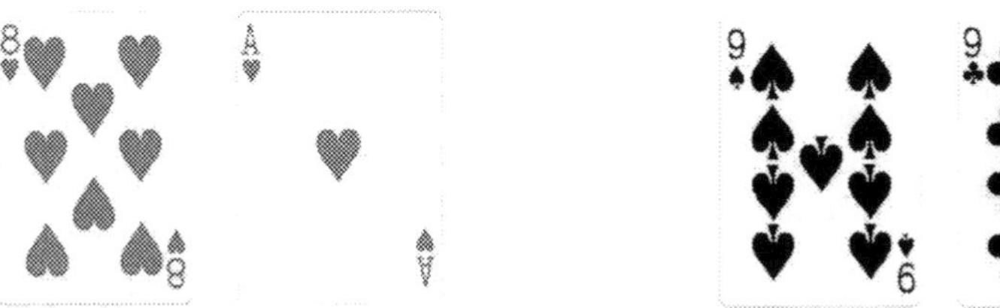

Player 1 _______________ Player 2 _______________

Player 3 _______________ Player 4 _______________

Which Player has the best hand and why?

____

Additional Exercises

Occasionally in Texas Hold'em Poker we come across hands that are deemed a draw. In these cases we are required to "split the pot".

Now that we have got used to looking at a few different types of hands with an outcome of a single winner, let's up the ante and have a go at working out which players will be sharing the spoils on the following exercises.

As with the first section of exercises use the same keys to identify each of the hands in the space provided then at the bottom of the page record the player that you feel would have won that round and the hand they received.

Hand	Key
High Card	HC
Pair	Pr
Two Pair	2P
Three of a Kind	3oK
Straight	Str
Flush	Fsh
Four of a Kind	4oK
Straight Flush	SFsh
Royal Flush	RFs

All answers can be found the Fish 'n' Chips Answer Guide on page 225.

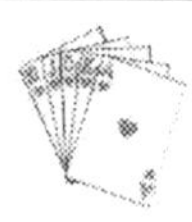

EXERCISE 1

Flop Turn River

Player 1 ______________ Player 2 ______________

Player 3 ______________ Player 4 ______________

Which Players have the best hands and why?

____

EXERCISE 2

Flop Turn River

Player 1 ______________

Player 2 ______________

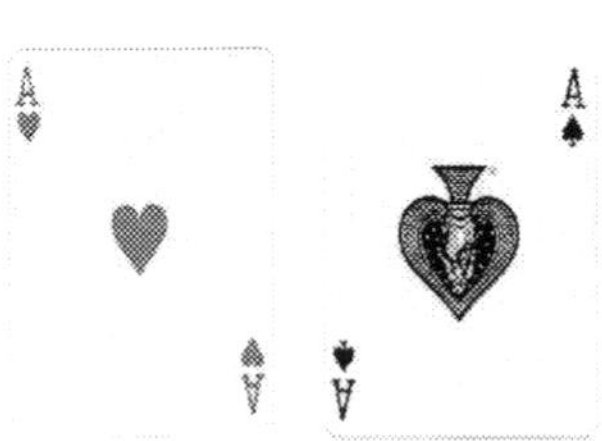

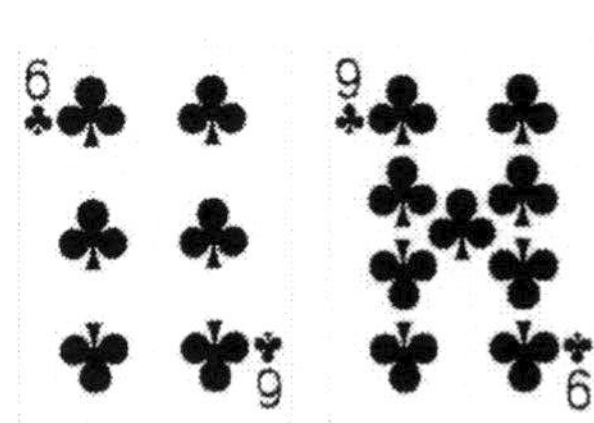

Player 3 ______________

Player 4 ______________

Which Players have the best hands and why?

____

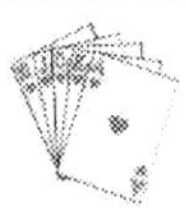

EXERCISE 3

Flop Turn River

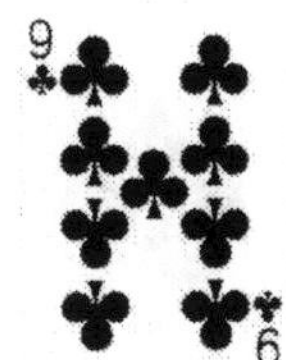

Player 1 ______________ Player 2 ______________

Player 3 ______________ Player 4 ______________

Which Players have the best hands and why?

____

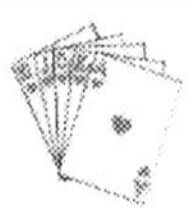

EXERCISE 4

Player 1 ______________

Player 2 ______________

Player 3 ______________

Player 4 ______________

Which Players have the best hands and why?

____

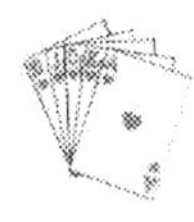

EXERCISE 5

Flop Turn River

Player 1 ______________ Player 2 ______________

Player 3 ______________ Player 4 ______________

Which Players have the best hands and why?

____

EXERCISE 6

Flop Turn River

Player 1 ______________ Player 2 ______________

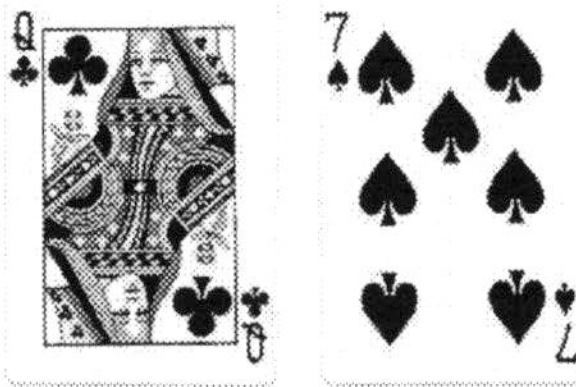

Player 3 ______________ Player 4 ______________

Which Players have the best hands and why?

____

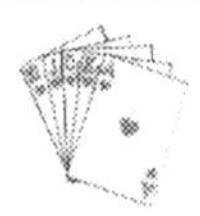

EXERCISE 7

Flop Turn River

Player 1 ______________

Player 2 ______________

Player 3 ______________

Player 4 ______________

Which Players have the best hands and why?

____

EXERCISE 8

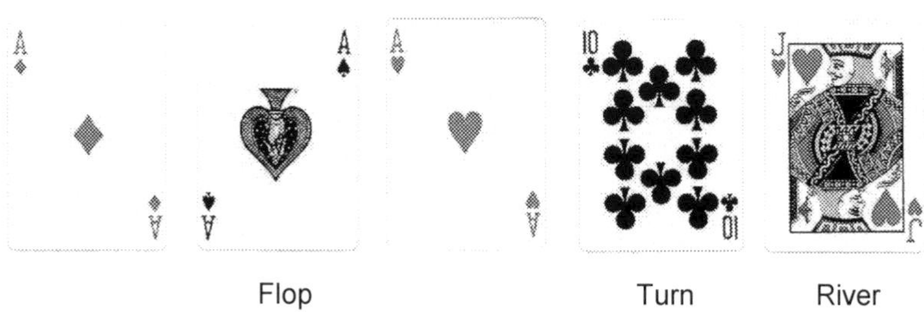

Flop Turn River

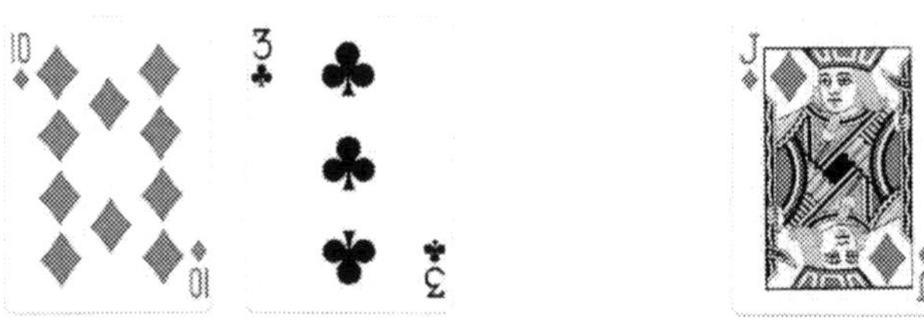

Player 1 ______________ Player 2 ______________

Player 3 ______________ Player 4 ______________

Which Players have the best hands and why?

____

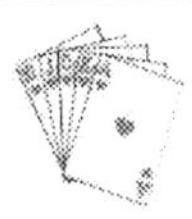

EXERCISE 9

Flop Turn River

Player 1 ______________

Player 2 ______________

Player 3 ______________

Player 4 ______________

Which Players have the best hands and why?

____

EXERCISE 10

Flop Turn River

Player 1 ______________

Player 2 ______________

Player 3 ______________

Player 4 ______________

Which Players have the best hands and why?

____

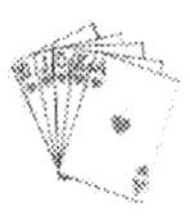

LESSON 4 - HOW TO PLAY

"Learning without thought is labour lost;
Thought without learning is perilous."

Confucius
(Chinese teacher, politician and philosopher)

Learning Outcomes

In Lesson 4 we will learn new terms and phrases as well as becoming familiar with the rules of Texas Hold'em. We are going to examine the rules and some of the general etiquette associated with the game.

Element 1: Terms to Get Us Started

Element 2: Playing the Game

Element 3: Poker Rules & Etiquette

3.1 Rules

3.2 Etiquette

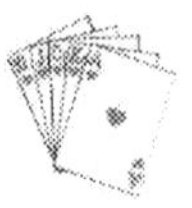

Element 1: Terms to Get Us Started

Betting - Any money wagered during the play of a hand.

Big Blind – Minimum Bet (forced).

Blinds - A type of forced bet, put into the pot before any of the cards are dealt.

Burn - To discard the top card from the deck, face down.

Call - To match the latest bet or raised amount.

Check - To continue playing without betting, provided no previous players have bet or raised.

Dealer – Player or person assigned responsibility for dealing the cards.

Fold – To discontinue playing in that hand.

Heads up - Only two players playing or remaining in a hand.

Hole Cards - The two cards you have been dealt.

Minimum bet – The minimum money or chips wagered during the play of a hand.

Misdeal – A deal which is ruined for some reason and must be re-dealt.

Post - To make the required small or big blind bet.

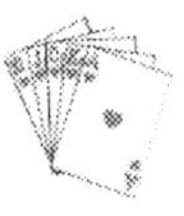

Rabbit hunting - Asking to see additional board cards after play is over.

Raise - To put in more money than the existing bet.

Showdown - When the cards are revealed at the end of the game.

Side pot - A separate pot created if one player has gone all-in and the other players continue to bet.

Small Blind – Half the minimum bet (forced).

Split Pot – Usually the result of a tie, each tied player takes an equal share.

Stack - A collection of 20 chips of the same denomination, usually arranged in an orderly column.

String Bet - A bet such that a player uses two separate motions to make a bet without verbally declaring their intention.

The Button - A token, usually white, used to mark the position of the dealer.

The Flop - The first three community cards dealt face up.

The River - The fifth (and last) community card dealt face up.

The Turn - The fourth community card dealt face up.

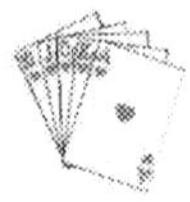

Element 2: Playing the Game

Texas Hold'em is played in nine simple stages:-

1. Blinds are posted.
2. Hole cards are dealt to each player.
3. A round of betting takes place.
4. The Flop.
5. A Second round of betting takes place.
6. The Turn.
7. A third round of betting takes place.
8. The River.
9. The final round of betting takes place.

As we progress through the nine stages, in the following example we will assume that there are nine players and that the Small Blind is 50 cents and the Big Blind (minimum bet) is $1.

D = Dealer

SB = Small Blind

BB = Big Blind

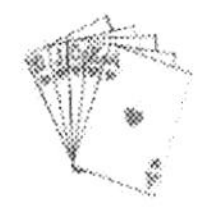

Stage 1 - Blinds Posted

To begin a new hand, two blind bets are posted. The player immediately to the left of the dealer posts the small blind which is half the minimum bet. The player to the left of the small blind posts the big blind which is equal to the minimum bet. The rest of the players do not put up any money to start the hand.

Because the deal rotates clockwise around the table at the start of every hand, each player will eventually act as the small blind, big blind and dealer.

Diagram 1 – Dealer & Blinds

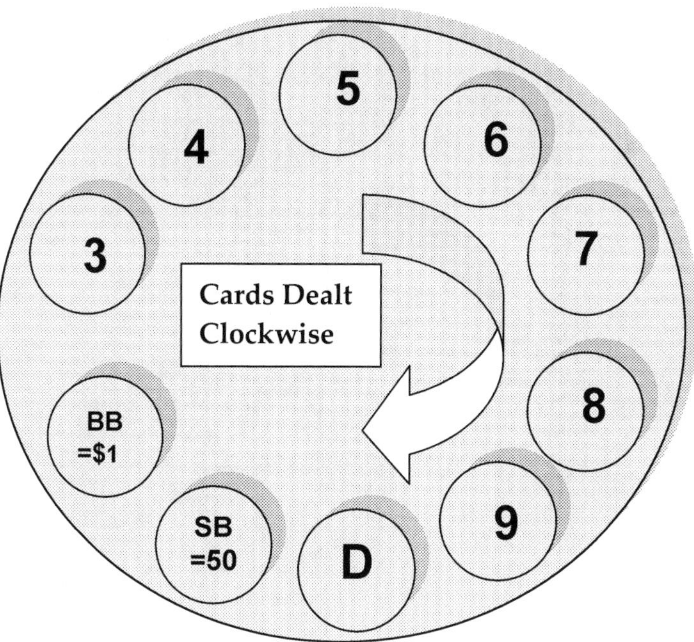

Stage 2 - Hole Cards Dealt

Each player is dealt two cards (hole cards) face down with the player in the small blind receiving the first card and the player with the "dealer button" getting the last card. These cards are dealt clockwise with each player receiving one card each followed by a second once all players have received their first card.

The deck is then placed face down in a single pile on the table in front the Dealer.

Stage 3 - First Round of Betting

The first betting round begins with the player to the left of the big blind (player 4) either putting in $1 to "call" the big blind bet or a minimum of $2 to "raise" the big blind. (In the first round of betting an initial raise must be at least double the size of the big blind). Alternatively, the player may discontinue by folding his hand.

The betting continues around the table in order with each player deciding to either fold, call the previous bet or re-raise until play reaches the player who posted the small blind. That player can then choose to fold, call the last bet or re-raise.

The last person to act is the player in the big blind position. If a player has raised then the big blind has the option to call, raise or fold. If no one has raised, then the big blind has the option to raise or just "check." Keep in mind that if the big blind raises, it must be a minimum of the value of the big blind. In the case where the big blind raises the pot, each player not already folded then has another opportunity to call, raise or fold. This sequence of betting continues until all players have either called the highest raise or folded.

In the following example track each point of play so that you fully understand how the bets have been made and the sequence of events that follows each player's decision. Use the diagrams to make notations through the following examples to help you keep track of the game progress. Don't forget that each player has the choice of calling, raising or folding.

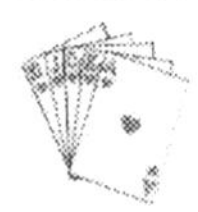

Diagram 2 – Hand Example

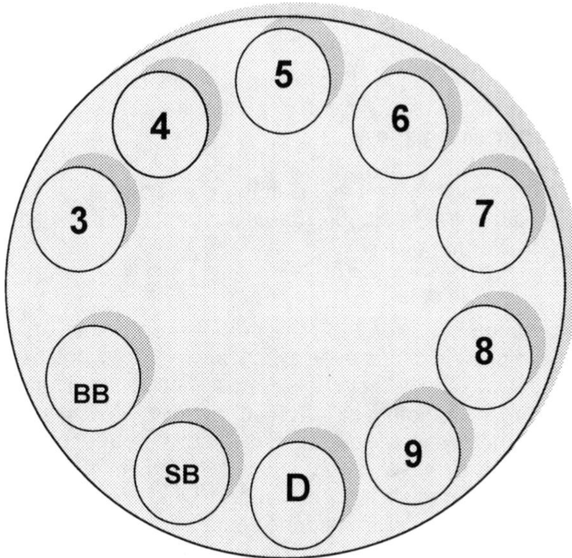

1. Small Blind posts 50c and Big Blind posts $1
2. Dealer deals the cards
3. Player 3 calls and puts in $1
4. Player 4 calls and puts in $1
5. Player 5 folds and can longer play in that hand
6. Player 6 folds
7. Player 7 calls and puts in $1
8. Players 8 and 9 both fold
9. Dealer raises to $3
10. Small blind calls and puts in $2.50 to match the bet. (SB had already put in 50c prior to the cards being dealt.)
11. Big blind folds and can longer play in that hand
12. Player 3 calls and puts in $2.
13. Player 4 calls and puts in $2
14. Players 5 & 6 have already folded so remain out of play

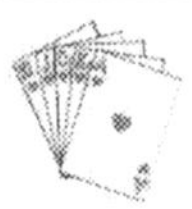

15. Player 7 now folds
16. Players 8 & 9 have already folded so remain out of play

Four players (SB, 3, 4 & D) remain involved in this hand and as such can continue to play into Stage 4 and 5 of the hand. To this point each remaining player has wagered $3.

Can you work out how much money is in the pot at this stage? *(Hint: Four players still remain in the hand, plus the initial bets of the BB and Player 7 who both folded after the dealer raised.)*

A couple of common mistakes can happen here. Some players in the Big Blind position fold their cards even when the pot has not been raised. They may have looked at their hole cards, decided that they are not particularly good and automatically folded when it was their turn to act. When a pot has not been raised the Big Blind is in effect getting a free look at the flop as they have already posted the minimum bet prior to the cards being dealt. As can sometimes happen, what are deemed to be bad hole cards can be suddenly transformed into a profitable hand after the flop.

A second common mistake made by beginners is folding their hands out of turn. This is something that should not be done under any circumstances as it gives an unfair advantage to players who have yet to play, as well as putting you out of a hand which may actually have proven to be a winning one. If a player knows another player is going to fold then the player with this information is in a position to act in such a way as to take a pot down without necessarily having to depend on the cards in his hand.

Stage 4 - The Flop

After the first betting round is completed, the dealer will “burn” the top card from the deck and then deal three cards face up in the middle of the table. This is known as the "Flop." These are community cards used by all the players to contribute to their hand.

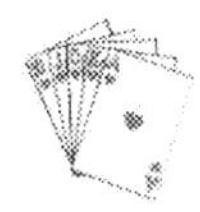

Stage 5 - Second Round of Betting

Did you calculate that the total pot to this stage would be $14? (Four players remain with each contributing $3, the Big Blind put $1 before folding as did Player 7.) Well done!

The second round of betting begins with the first active player to the left of the dealer button. In the case of our example, this would be the small blind. The minimum bet for this round is $1.

Diagram 3 – Hand Example 2

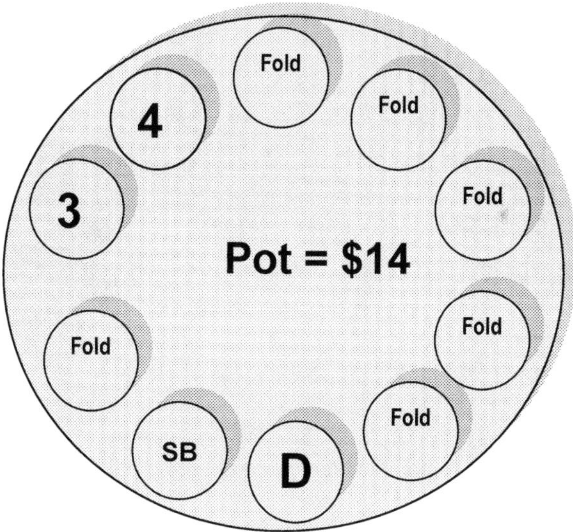

1. The small blind is now first to act and checks
2. Player 3, next to act, also checks
3. Player 4 bets $1
4. Dealer raises to $3

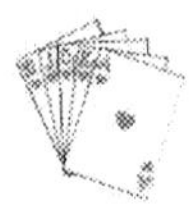

5. Small blind folds
6. Player 3 calls and puts in $3
7. Player 4 calls and puts in $2 (already bet $1)

Three players (3, 4 & Dealer) remain involved in this hand and as such can continue to play into Stages 6 and 7 of the hand. To this point each remaining player has wagered $6.

Can you work out how much money is in the pot at this stage? *(Hint: Starting pot plus three remaining players who have each bet in this round.)*

Stage 6 - The Turn

Once the second betting round is completed, the dealer burns another card and then turns a fourth card face up in the middle of the table. This is called the "Turn."

Players now have a total of six cards to make a standard five card poker hand. (Two hole cards and four community cards).

Stage 7 - Third Round of Betting

Did you calculate that the total pot to this stage would be $23? (Starting pot of $14 plus the three remaining players contributing a further $3 each.)

Our third round of betting now begins with the first active player to the left of the dealer button being Player 3. The minimum bet for this round again remains at 1$.

Diagram 4 – Hand Example 3

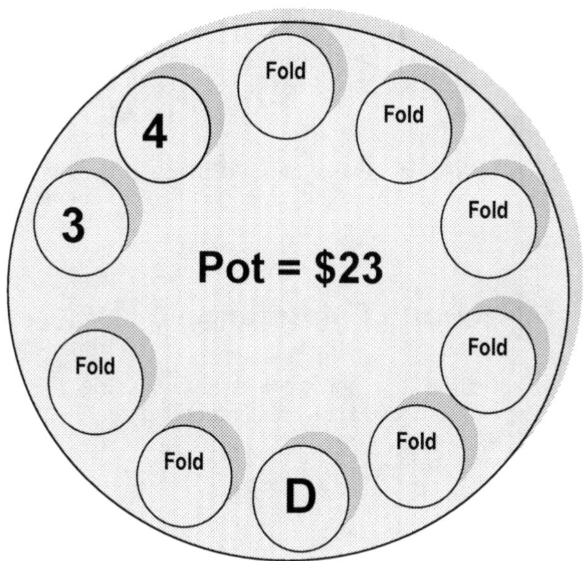

1. Player 3, now first to act, checks
2. Player 4 also checks
3. Dealer raises to $3
4. Player 3 calls and puts in $3
5. Player 4 folds

Two players (3 & Dealer) remain involved in this hand and can continue to play into Stages 8 and 9 of the hand. To this point each remaining player has wagered $9.

Can you work out how much money is in the pot at this stage? *(Hint: Previous pot plus the two remaining players who have each bet in this round.)*

Stage 8 - The River

Following the third round of betting the dealer will again burn a card then turn the fifth and final community card face up in the middle of the table. This is called the "River". You will quite often hear the phrase “to drown on the river”. One of the great aspects of Texas Hold’em poker is the way the strength of your hand can change from moment to moment. From a winning hand to a losing hand or from a losing one to a winning one, based on that “river “card .

Players now have a total of seven cards to make a standard five card Texas Hold’em poker hand. (Two hole cards and five community cards.)

Stage 9 - Final Round of Betting

Did you calculate that the total pot to this stage would be $29? (Starting pot of $23 plus the two remaining players contributing a further $3 each.)

Diagram 5 – Hand Example 4

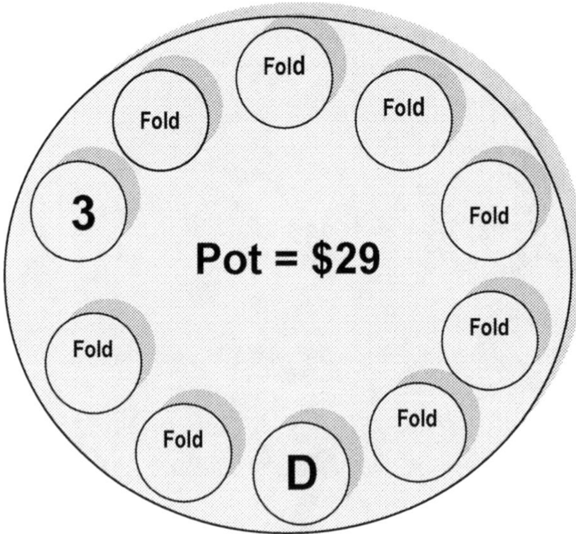

Our fourth and final round of betting is now ready to begin. In the case of our example, the active player to the left of the dealer button is 3. The minimum bet for this round remains at 1$.

As there are only two players remaining, we are now at "Heads up".

1. Player 3 raises to $12
2. Dealer Calls and puts in $12

The pot now contains $53 and play moves into the showdown. Both players now show their cards to determine the winner based on the standard poker hands that we have already discussed in previous lessons.

Research Question 3

Why does Johnny Chan
keep an orange at the table?

Element 3: The Rules & Etiquette

3.1 Rules

Many tournaments both live and on-line have varied rules and regulations but there are certainly a few basic rules and expected standards that are common to all. It is a very good idea to become familiar with these. If you are about to enter any tournament you should ensure that you understand the expectations surrounding that competition.

Let's start by looking at some of the basic rules.

1. If it is your turn to act and you make a verbal declaration, (call, raise or fold) then provided you have the chips to do so, you are required to follow through with the action. A verbal declaration overrides any physical action. For example, if you put $20 into the pot and declare a raise of $30, then you will be required to put in the extra $10. Any action taken out of turn is not binding however, this is not considered fair play and you may be penalised depending on the local rules.

2. String bets are forbidden. A string bet is either when a player uses more than one forward motion to put chips in for a raise without verbally declaring the raise first or when a player verbally states, "I see your call...and I raise", without putting the full bet in first. String bets are problematic because they are confusing and ambiguous.

3. Split pots will be divided as evenly as possible. If chips cannot be broken down any further then the remaining chips shall be passed to the player who is in the worst position.

4. When a side pot is present at "showdown" the player who is all-in can only win the pot that has been set aside for them.

5. Players must post blinds and antes before the hole cards are dealt. If a player does not have enough chips to cover the requirement then a side pot will be created.

6. The big blind must always be posted. (How the blinds are posted when players have been eliminated will be explained in later lessons.)

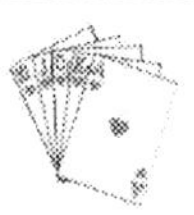

7. All of the players' chips must be displayed at all times and the highest denomination chips must be visible for all other players to see.

8. A player may call the clock on another player that is deemed to be taking an unreasonable amount of time to play.

9. A player must be in their seat and ready to play by the time all other preceding players have acted, otherwise that player's hand will be deemed to be dead (folded).

10. If your cards touch the "muck" pile (cards that have been discarded) they will be ruled dead.

11. Disclosing the contents of your hand will result in your hand being deemed dead.

12. Advising another player how to play a hand is not permitted.

13. Discussing discarded cards while a hand is still in play is not permitted.

14. If the dealer exposes any card during the deal then that deal is to be regarded as a misdeal.

15. If a player deliberately exposes cards during play then that player's hand will be deemed to be dead. Each player in the hand has the right to know what the cards were and can request to be informed as to the contents of the dead player's hand.

16. At showdown, players begin to show their cards starting from the left of the last person to call and any player can then "muck" his cards if they cannot win.

17. Players may show their cards to spectators.

18. During a hand, players are not allowed to discuss their hands with anyone including spectators.

19. If a deck becomes marked it should be changed immediately.

20. Rabbit hunting is forbidden. (Viewing the remaining board cards after the hand has finished.)

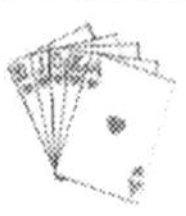

3.2 Etiquette

I know for the most part these points on etiquette are going to be self-explanatory for most readers however, I would still like to touch on them as playing in a manner that is "sportsmanlike" really is a big part of playing poker.

1. **Be polite.**
   It is important that we always try to remain friendly and polite when sitting at the poker table. Not only is it simply the right way to behave, but it also helps to keep your mind focussed on the job at hand – winning poker. The moment we start using bad language or profanities we lose that focus and credibility which will only bring negativity to your game. Discussions about politics and religion can very quickly become heated and as such, should really be avoided. Try to keep your conversations upbeat and light.

2. **Don't cheat.**
   I have only one opinion when it comes to cheating. It is for losers. If, for whatever reason, you are not capable of playing an honest game, then in short - don't play. Cheating will destroy friendships and poker relationships and is completely unnecessary.

3. **Don't criticise.**
   Criticism is something I have been guilty of on more than one occasion and it is something that I do have to work on. One of the joys (or frustrations, depending on your outlook on life) of poker is that we come up against players from all walks of life and with varying levels of skill. The result of this is that we will often be faced with plays that make little or no sense to us. It is when confronted with this situation that we need to remind ourselves that players have their own reasons for doing what they do. Once again avoiding criticism keeps us focussed on the game and helps us to avoid the mental hole that can compromise our own game plan.

4. **Be organised**.
I have to admit that I love to be organised at the poker table. I like to see my chips stacked neatly and when I play "there is a place for everything and everything in its place". Organisation helps us to keep track of our own chip stack, it helps to keep the game running in an orderly fashion and keeps other players happy who are paying attention. (They can see how many more chips you have than they do!)

5. **Play at a reasonable speed.**
Playing 500 while serving in the Royal Australian Navy, we used to have a saying, "a quick game is a good game". Texas Hold'em is no exception. It is good to sit down to a game where the pace is reasonable and the players are paying attention.

6. **Be courteous.**
To remain courteous during the game, when winning or losing is a sign of maturity and self control. Poker can be a very contentious and trying game and it is very easy to have momentary lapses. One thing that you need to remind yourself of when confronted with the urge to lose your cool is that this is one small moment in time with regard to your poker "career". You will be playing hundreds (if not thousands) more hands and if you take the opportunity to control your feelings during play, your game will only improve.

7. **Stay focussed.**
Don't become distracted while at the table. Talking or texting on your mobile phone does not do anyone any favours and is really not productive. Eating and drinking at the table is acceptable within reason. Chowing down on a pizza while sitting at a poker table is probably not going to win you any friends though. Especially if you are getting sauce over everything, so use a bit of common sense when it comes to food and drink.

8. **Be patient.**
   Each game you sit down to is going to be made up of a variety of individuals whether you are playing on-line or face to face. Each player will be bringing their own skill sets and baggage to the table. As such we need to demonstrate a little patience with our opponents. In addition we might not be hitting our cards and the game may not be going our way. It is times like these when another lapse in judgement can cost us our reputation, a game or a load of cash.

9. **Don't play under the influence.**
   Playing under the influence of alcohol or drugs is the easiest way to go broke. It is also one of the best ways to ensure that your game and skill level won't develop and move forward. Let alone being insulting to other players who wish to have an enjoyable game. If you are playing under the influence, your judgement is impaired and your game is jeopardised. You are a target and over time will lose more than you win. If you are serious about poker keep your mind clear.

10. **Be mentally prepared.**
    If you enter a game and you are prepared mentally (i.e. you are in the mood and feeling good) then you will be in a position to be on top of your game. If however, you are entering the game worrying about issues such as your job, personal life, money or any of the other problems which seem to consume our lives these days, then you may struggle to play and participate to your best of your ability. I must say this one is a big ask but definitely one of the most important. I admit that I often play with "life" cramming my game – most definitely another aspect of my game that needs work.

Now that we have prepared ourselves for the game at hand by understanding the rules and have got ourselves into a frame of mind that is ready for action – Let's Play! Well almost - but not quite yet. We still have a couple more points we need to cover before we get into a game.

For now I would like to conduct a little review exercise, so sharpen that pencil and let's see how much you have learned to this point.

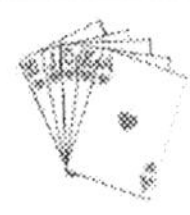

LESSON 5 - LET'S REVIEW

"Every new horizon begins with a branch of education"

Greg Evans
(American cartoonist)

Learning Outcomes

In Lessons 1 – 4 we have come to understand our goals and reasons for playing, the hand structures, rules and few of the things we should and should not do while sitting at a poker table. Now let's have a bit of fun and see how much you have retained.

Element 1: Multiple Choice Quiz
Element 2: Short Answer Questions
Element 3: Crossword

All answers can be found the Fish 'n' Chips Answer Guide on page 227.

Research Question 4

What's the nickname of Chris Ferguson?

Element 1: Multiple Choice Quiz

Try and answer the following questions by placing the letter of your choice in the box provided. If you are unsure please review the previous lessons.

1. What item indicates that a player is now the dealer?

   (A) The Zip
   (B) The Plate
   (C) The Button
   (D) The Octopus

2. When placing a bet, this type of bet is considered illegal?

   (A) Rope bet
   (B) Nail bet
   (C) String bet
   (D) Royal bet

3. In the acronym SMART the "S" stands for what?

   (A) Specific
   (B) Super
   (C) Silly
   (D) Simple

4. The highest ranked hand you can win with in poker is what?

   (A) Straight Flush
   (B) Royal Flush
   (C) Flush
   (D) Four of a kind

5. A-A is also known as what?

   (A) Guns
   (B) Cannons
   (C) Bombs
   (D) Bullets

6. Four of a kind is also known as what?

   (A) Trips
   (B) Quads
   (C) Hijack
   (D) Twisters

7. What is the name given to the card that determines the winner of a tied hand?
   (A) Community Card
   (B) Tie Breaker
   (C) Killer
   (D) Kicker

8. How many cards are "community" cards?
   (A) 2
   (B) 3
   (C) 4
   (D) 5

9. The last card to be dealt into the community cards is called what?
   (A) The Stream
   (B) The Ocean
   (C) The River
   (D) The Creek

10. Which word does not belong with the others?
    (A) Call
    (B) Fold
    (C) Raise
    (D) Chip

11. To be known as a bad player is also to be known as a what?
    (A) Camel
    (B) Donkey
    (C) Sheep
    (D) Goat

12. These were once made from ivory, bone and wood.
    (A) Fish
    (B) Coins
    (C) Chips
    (D) Cards

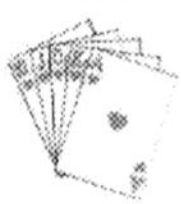

Element 2: Short Answer Questions

Please try to answer all of the following 10 questions in the area provided. If you are unsure please review the previous lessons.

1. "Don't tap on the aquarium" means what?

2. What is the quote, "The harder I work, the more I have of it" referring to?

3. "Over cards" are what?

4. What is the only circumstance where more than one player can get a Royal Flush?

5. What two cards are referred to as a "Royal Marriage"?

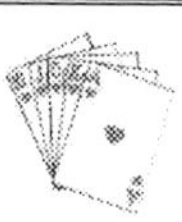

6. When considering the “Kicker”, do we ever count a sixth card or seventh card?

7. Is there ever a circumstance when we don’t post a “Big Blind”?

8. The Small Blind is usually what size in relation to the Big Blind?

9. Can you show spectators your hand during play?

10. Under what circumstances should we immediately replace a deck of cards?

Element 3: Crossword

Have fun with this crossword. If you are unsure please review the previous lessons.

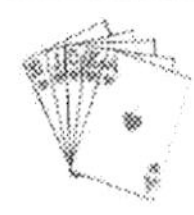

Clues - Across

1 - 4-of-a-kind

3 - To pass or not bet.

5 - The first three community cards dealt face up.

9 - A deal which is ruined for some reason and must be redealt.

11 - The set of face up community cards

12 - What s used to determine a winner when hands are tied. This will be explained in greater detail in this chapter through the examples provided.

14 - To discontinue playing in that hand

16 - A token, usually white, used to mark the position of the dealer.

18 - Placing bets with more than one motion without verbally declaring your intention

19 - The fifth community card dealt face up

20 - Usually the result of a tie, each player tied takes an equal share.

21 - To discard the top card from the deck, face down.

22 Cards - A card dealt face-up to the center of the table that can be used by all players in the action.

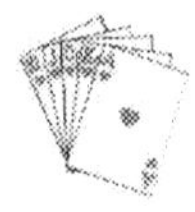

Clues – Down

2 - Player or person assigned responsibility for dealing the cards.

4 - To match the latest bet or raised amount.

6 - To make the required small or big blind bet.

7 - Any money wagered during the play of a hand.

8 - A type of forced bet, put into the pot before any of the cards are dealt.

10 - Only two players playing or remaining

11 - Full House

13 Cards - The two cards you have been dealt.

15 cards - A community card with a higher rank than any player's pocket pair

17 - The fourth community card dealt face up.

20 Pot - Usually the result of a tie, each player tied takes an equal share.

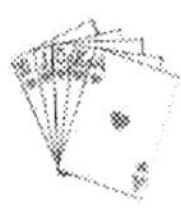

LESSON 6 - THREE IMPORTANT FACTORS

A good beginning makes a good end."

Louis L'Amour
(American author)

Learning Outcomes

When we are playing poker there are a multitude of factors that go into the decision-making process. If it were as simple as calculating one or two equations or mixing a couple of ingredients into a pot and coming up with a result then the world would be full of professional players. I am not proclaiming to be a professional poker player and there are a lot of them out there who can teach you the finer details of poker through their wisdom and experience.

What I can do however, is give you some basic guidance so that at least you have a place to start. A foundation, if you like, and by keeping it simple to begin with your game will improve.

There are three important factors that help us make decisions with regard to which hands we should be playing and which hands we should be avoiding. In order of relevance these are:-

1. The cards we are holding;
2. The amount of chips we possess in a game; and
3. Our relative position at the table in relation to the other players.

In this lesson we are going to learn about each of these factors and later incorporate what we have learned into a few practise games. We will also be concluding this lesson with a quick look at some starting hands to consider playing or avoiding.

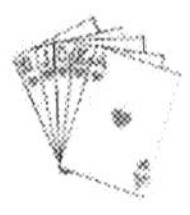

Element 1: Terms to Get Us Started

Element 2: Cards You Possess

- **2.1 169 Possibilities**
- **2.2 Top 10 Best Hands**
- **2.3 Worst Starting Hands**
- **2.4 Hands and Ranks**
- **2.5 Common Hand Names**
- **2.6 Common Hole Card Names**

Element 3: Chip Stack

Element 4: Table Position

Element 5: Starting Hands to Play

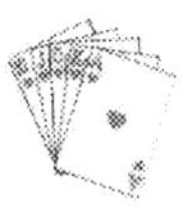

Element 1: Terms to Get Us Started

Bully - To continuously bluff, or a player who does so, usually because of a superior stack size or position.

Drawing hands - To stay in a hand because it offers the possibility of improving, usually to a straight or flush.

Levels - The type of game a player should be playing according to that players bankroll

Nut/s - To hold the best hand.

Odds - the probability that something is or will occur, or is more likely to occur than something else.

Range - The group of hands a player is likely to play

Short stack - A number of chips that is relatively low compared to the other players at the table.

Steal - usually means to bluff.

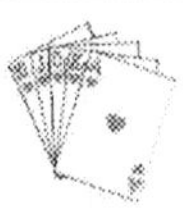

Element 2: Cards You Possess

2.1 169 Possibilities

As we know, there are 13 cards in each suit, Ace to King. As each player begins with two hole cards, a simple calculation of 13 x 13 = 169 possible two-card starting hands. Hands of equal rank but different suits do not count.

For example, an Ace and King of hearts has the same value as the Ace and King of spades, clubs or diamonds. Unlike some other card games, Texas Hold'em does not have a rank structure for the suits and they are all deemed to be equal.

Of these 169 starting hands there are only about 75 that are considered profitable to play and this is where the question becomes complicated.

Which hands do we play and when?

I would like to begin by running through the hands that are considered to be the top playable hands. We will then examine some of the hands that are considered to be unprofitable.

When playing in tournaments, whether on-line or live, you will generally begin at a table with 9 or 10 players. It is not my intention here to suggest that you only play or don't play a specific hand because there are factors that affect what and when we should play. I do however, want to pass on to you what most professionals agree to be a good starting point.

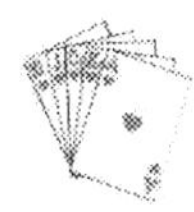

2.2 Top 10 Best Hands

1. A-A

Oh those Aces! The very thought fills me with a mix of dread and adrenaline-charged anticipation. A-A, otherwise known as American Airlines, pocket rockets or bullets. This is the hand we all dream of hitting. Without exception, I get a knot in my stomach when I get this hand, not only because it is the most powerful starting hand but because it is also a hand that you can lose a large amount of money on. Rightly or wrongly, it is the only hand that I have never folded pre-flop. And yes, I have been stung severely because I have not let it go when I should have, post-flop.

The odds of receiving a pair of aces are 220 to 1. Having said that, I was playing in an on-line tournament in 2011 and was dealt four pairs of aces over the spread of ten hands. (Incidentally, I won them all - screen grabbed the action and sent it to all the people I play poker with.) I daresay I may never see a run of hands like that again but it does go to show that anything can happen in the world of poker.

2. K-K

We all love to see those Cowboys, Elvis Presley, King Kong and as the second to best starting hand it remains very strong. These two cards will win you a great deal over your playing career. You must always be wary if upon seeing the flop an ace falls, as this can and will on occasion cost you dearly. You must be prepared to let go and move on.

Like a pair of aces, the odds of receiving a pair of kings is also 220 to 1 but unlike aces I have folded these occasionally pre-flop, (though very rarely).

3. Q-Q

A pair of queens (my wife's favourite hand) is a very good starting hand. Whilst kings and aces still dominate, you have a very good starting hand compared to Jacks and below. A pair of queens is generally known as ladies.

Like aces and kings, the chances of getting queens is 220 to 1 and again I will fold this hand pre-flop depending on the circumstances of the hand I

am involved in. I must admit though, I still on occasion fall in love with these cards and refuse to let them go when alarm bells are screaming. Probably one of the reasons I am not play professionally as yet!

4. A-K

Anna Kournikova (looks good but rarely wins). More commonly known as Big Slick, Ace-King is a great starting hand, and will always give you a rush when you hold it. It is the strongest of the drawing hands. You really need the flop to hit an ace or king giving you top pair or two cards to a straight for it to become profitable. Suited it is slightly stronger because it means you may be drawing to the nut flush. But never forget, this can be a very tricky hand to play.

As far as beginners are concerned, this hand can get costly because they find it difficult to throw away when they don't hit the flop. As with A-A and K-K I have both won and lost various amounts in cash games and tournaments with this hand. The chance of being dealt an A-K unsuited is 110 to 1 and suited is 331 to 1.

5. J-J

There is a saying among poker players when it comes to being dealt this hand - "There are three ways to play Jacks – check, raise or fold, and they are all wrong".

Jacks are a very tricky hand to play and once again as a beginner you need to be very wary of how, when and where you play this hand. If the flop shows a queen, king or an ace, you need to be cautious and play accordingly. Jacks are known as Fishhooks, Hooks, Jokers, or Johnnies and the odds of being dealt a pair of Jacks are 220 to 1.

6. A-Q

Ace-Queen is the second best drawing hand, and still a great hand to start with but caution is advised. This hand is known as Little Slick, Big Chick or Mrs. Slick and like A-K the odds of receiving this hand are the same, unsuited 110 to 1 and suited is 331 to 1.

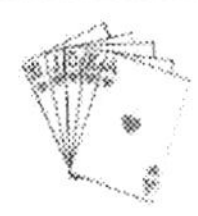

7. K-Q

King-Queen, especially suited, is a great drawing hand and with this hand you are only worried that an ace may fall on the board. K-Q suited is known as a royal marriage while K-Q unsuited is referred to as the mixed marriage. In addition, K-Q of hearts is often called Valentine's Day. The odds of receiving this hand are the same as A-K and A-Q.

8. A-J

Ace-Jack is another great drawing hand. Suited hands are better and this is no exception, but unsuited still remains playable. A-J is referred to as Blackjack, Ajax or Jackass.

9. K-J

Commonly known as Kojak or King John and when unsuited (J-K off suit) is also known as the bachelor hand (think about it!!). It is a nice starting hand and an even more attractive proposition when suited. This hand still remains inferior to the hands we mentioned previously so beware when confronted with big raises or life and death tournament decisions. From what I have read, most professionals stay clear of this hand as it creates a false sense of superiority.

10. A-10

Ace-Ten is another good hand - in fact it is one of my favourite hands when suited. You have an ace and it comes with a decent kicker but caution is once again advised, there are still stronger hands out there. A-10 is known as Johnny Moss, A-Team or Bookends.

2.3 The Worst Starting Hands

1. 2-7

Coming in at position 169 is the 7-2 off suit and it is this hand that is considered the worst starting hand in Texas Hold'em. This pair of cards is the lowest two cards you can be dealt that cannot make a straight on the

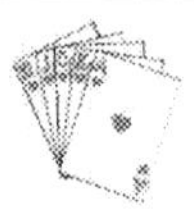

flop as four cards are required between 2 and 7. In the event that you receive these cards suited, you are still only aiming for a very low flush and the pairs you may make are also low.

This hand is best thrown away especially as a beginner as it will only cost you money in most cases. This hand is referred to as "The Hammer" and when suited, the velvet hammer.

2. 8-2, 8-3

Chuck, fold, dump or let go – either way with these card is good. However you want to phrase it, these hands (off suit) at 168 and 167 really are no-brainers when it comes to decision time - to play or not to play. Even suited these hands are generally dogs and I actually feel quite relieved at times when I receive hands of this nature because no decision is required. An auto-fold (unless bluffing) but for the moment we shall just leave it at that.

3. 9-2, 9-3 and 9-4

Positioned at 166, 165, and 164 respectively, these hands will not produce straights with all five community cards in play and generally speaking the only reasonable feature of these hands is the fact that they contain a 9. Having said that, even if you hit a 9 on the flop you still may be up against hands of greater strength and as such, you should fold these once again. Even if you are given the opportunity to get a free flop you should still play with caution and not invest a great deal.

4. 2-6

At 163 this hand loses most of the time and is another hand that should not be played in most circumstances. In short it should be relegated to the rubbish pile unless the opportunity for free cards is present.

6. 2-10

This hand is famous because Doyle Brunson, a master among poker players, captured two World Series of Poker Bracelets with it. So, the hand was named after him. With 161 hands sitting in better positions than

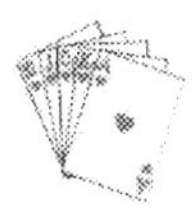

this one, like the previous hands mentioned, it should be thrown out in most cases and viewed as another losing prospect.

7. 7-3, 10-3

Simply rubbish. The reasons for not playing these two hands suited or not remains similar to the hands already discussed. 3-7 are called "Hachem" and are so named after the legendary Australian poker player Joe Hachem. He won the 2005 World Series of Poker Main Event and a $7.5 million prize with this hand when he flopped a straight.

8. Ugly cards continue.

I have included a chart at the end of this section so that you can see which cards continue to represent losing or poor risk propositions.

9. Face card + low card, unsuited

One of the most common mistakes beginners make is that when they see a face (picture) card they think that they are good to go. Paint (any picture card) represents half a hand and without a decent kicker as in the hands I have already described, you are literally half way to a loss if you decide to play on. When played, these types of hands may win you the occasional pot but generally speaking, over time they are going to cost you a lot more than you have won. So again avoid the "traps for young players" and stay away from them.

10. Ace + low card, unsuited

Another monumental mistake made by beginners, playing any ace. They do win occasionally, and it is a little demoralising when you fold an ace with a low kicker only to see the flop come down favourably. However, you must remember that to win over time you must be playing the right hands consistently and aces with low kickers do not win over the long run.

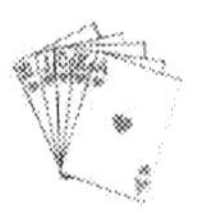

2.4 Hands and Ranks

The following chart indicates the possible 169 starting hands and their corresponding rank. You may find some variations in this ranking through the course of your reading, surfing and general poker education but generally it is an accurate representation of where all hands fit in relation to each other.

I have included this chart more for interest sake however, I feel it is a good idea to at least memorise the first 20 ranks and their corresponding hands fit in the scheme of things. There are two reasons I suggest you memorise these hands.

The first is because when I started to play, I found that I often overplayed hands because of the nice paint (K-Jo for example). Secondly, I simply fell in love with an Ace and found it hard to let go. Without a clear understanding in my head as to which hands were ranked higher, I often played hands that looked good but seldom paid out.

The second reason I suggest you take this approach is that if you have a good understanding of hand strength, it means you can focus on other aspects of the game. More importantly, you will then have time to formulate ideas as to how you will play in certain positions at certain times, without the need to continually concentrate on your hand strength.

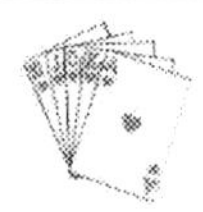

Diagram 6 – Hand Ranks

Note: s = suited; o = off suit (not suited)

Rank	Hand
1	A-A
2	K-K
3	Q-Q
4	A-Ks
5	J-J
6	A-Qs
7	K-Qs
8	A-Js
9	K-Js
10	10-10
11	A-Ko
12	A-10s
13	Q-Js
14	K-10s
15	Q-10s
16	J-10s
17	9-9
18	A-Qo
19	A-9s
20	K-Qo
21	8-8
22	K-9s

Rank	Hand
23	10-9s
24	A-8s
25	Q-9s
26	J-9s
27	A-Jo
28	A-5s
29	7-7
30	A-7s
31	K-Jo
32	A-4s
33	A-3s
34	A-6s
35	Q-Jo
36	6-6
37	K-8s
38	10-8s
39	A-2s
40	9-8s
41	J-8s
42	A-10o
43	Q-8s
44	K-7s

Rank	Hand
45	K-10o
46	5-5
47	J-10o
48	8-7s
49	Q-10o
50	4-4
51	3-3
52	2-2
53	K-6s
54	9-7s
55	K-5s
56	7-6s
57	10-7s
58	K-4s
59	K-2s
60	K-3s
61	Q-7s
62	8-6s
63	6-5s
64	J-7s
65	5-4s
66	Q-6s

Rank	Hand
67	7-5s
68	9-6s
69	Q-5s
70	6-4s
71	Q-4s
72	Q-3s
73	10-9o
74	10-6s
75	Q-2s
76	A-9o
77	5-3s
78	8-5s
79	J-6s
80	J-9o
81	K-9o
82	J-5s
83	Q-9o
84	4-3s
85	7-4s
86	J-4s
87	J-3s
88	9-5s

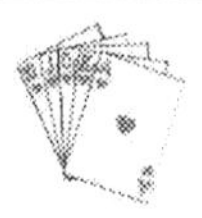

Rank	Hand
89	J-2s
90	6-3s
91	A-8o
92	5-2s
93	10-5s
94	8-4s
95	10-4s
96	10-3s
97	4-2s
98	10-2s
99	9-8o
100	10-8o
101	A-5o
102	A-7o
103	7-3s
104	A-4o
105	3-2s
106	9-4s
107	9-3s
108	J-8o
109	A-3o

Rank	Hand
110	6-2s
111	9-2s
112	K-8o
113	A-6o
114	8-7o
115	Q-8o
116	8-3s
117	A-2o
118	8-2s
119	9-7o
120	7-2s
121	7-6o
122	K-7o
123	6-5o
124	10-7o
125	K-6o
126	8-6o
127	5-4o
128	K-5o
129	J-7o
130	7-5o

Rank	Hand
131	Q-7o
132	K-4o
133	K-3o
134	9-6o
135	K-2o
136	6-4o
137	Q-6o
138	5-3o
139	8-5o
140	10-6o
141	Q-5o
142	4-3o
143	Q-4o
144	Q-3o
145	7-4o
146	Q-2o
147	J-6o
148	6-3o
149	J-5o
150	9-5o
151	5-2o

Rank	Hand
152	J-4o
153	J-3o
154	4-2o
155	J-2o
156	8-4o
157	10-5o
158	10-4o
159	3-2o
160	10-3o
161	7-3o
162	10-2o
163	6-2o
164	9-4o
165	9-3o
166	9-2o
167	8-3o
168	8-2o
169	7-2o

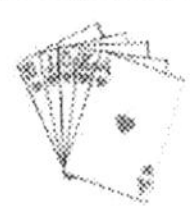

Throughout this book I have begun each lesson exploring the terminology and in Lesson 11 - Learning the Language, we will be talking a closer look at poker language. For now though, I would like to take a look at some of the common (slang) names associated with the hands we are going to become very familiar with. Although not a definitive list, I have covered 10 common hand names as well as 25 of the most of the common hole card slang names.

2.5 Common Hand Names

1. Straight flush, ace to five - Steel wheel
2. Four of a kind - Book, Case, Quads
3. Four of a kind, aces - Four Pips
4. Full house - Full boat, Boat,
5. Flush of hearts or diamonds - Pink, All Pink
6. Flush of clubs or spades - Blue, All Blue
7. Flush of clubs - Puppy Feet, Puppy Toes
8. Straight, ten to ace – Broadway
9. Straight, ace to five - Wheel, Bicycle, Bike
10. Three of a kind – Trips or Set. A Set refers to a player who holds two cards in the hand and one on the board where as trips is when two cards appear on the board and a player holds one card.

2.6 Common Hole Card Names

A-A.............Pocket Rockets, American Airlines, Bullets,
K-K ....Cowboys, Elvis Presley, King Kong
Q-Q ....Cowgirls, Ladies
J-J ....Fishhooks, Hooks, Jokers, Johnnies
A-K ....Big Slick, Anna Kournikova, Machine Gun
A-Q ....Little Slick, Big Chick, Mrs. Slick
A-J ....Blackjack, Ajax, Jackass
A-10...........(A-T) Johnny Moss, A-Team, Bookends
K-Q ....Marriage, Royalty
K-J ....Kojak, King John
K-9.............Canine, Dog, the Donk
Q-J.............Maverick
Q-10...........(Q-T) Q-Tip
J-10............Cloutier
10-10 ....(TT) TNT, Dimes, Boxcars
9-9 ....Wayne Gretzky, German virgin
8-8 ....Snowmen, Octopussy, Infinities
7-7 ....Hockey Sticks, Candy Canes, Walking Sticks
6-6 ....Route 66
5-5 ....Presto, Nickels, Speed Limit
4-4 ....Sailboats
3-3 ....Crabs, Hooters
2-2 ....Ducks, Swans, Sleepers
7-2 ....The hammer (off suit)
7-2 ....Velvet hammer (suited)

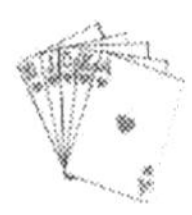

Element 3: Chip Stack

Whether you are playing cash games or tournaments, knowing the size of your own chip stack and that of other players is vital. This information will affect not only how you play but also how other players at your table play.

Stack size can allow you to become a 'bully', change your 'range' of playable hands or simply affect your mental state and contribute to your decision-making process.

Important note about cash games!!

When you enter a cash game it will generally have a maximum buy-in. Quite often, especially on-line, the buy-in is 100 big blinds. If the blinds are 10c/20c then the maximum allowable buy-in for that game will be $20. It is important that you always enter a cash game with the maximum buy-in allowable. (Providing you do not exceed bankroll requirements which will be discussed in Lesson 7).

In other words you are joining the game by putting yourself in the most powerful position you can be in with relation to your own stack size. Quite often I play games and see players join games with half or even a third of the maximum buy-in. Immediately this tells me they are either playing above their level (which will be discussed later) or they are not sure what they should be doing. In either case that player is telling me they are vulnerable and as such I will take advantage of that information.

Research Question 5

Who do the four Kings in a deck of cards represent?

LARGE CHIP STACK

Having a large stack size is awesome and a wonderful position to be in and although you may think the advantages obvious, I would like to mention several points you need to consider.

Advantages:

1. It allows you to be the bully – You are now able to push other players into situations they are not comfortable with or force them to make decisions that under different circumstances they would avoid.

2. It allows you to bluff more often and open up your hand range because of the fear factor associated with your stack size.

3. Depending on the overall situation it may allow you to relax more and play fewer hands, cruise to the end of a day's play, ensure you make the final table or simply give you time to re-group your thoughts and contemplate strategies.

Disadvantages

Beware, a large stack size can also have its draw backs. You need to be conscious of issues such as:-

1. Getting Chip Drunk. Like the distant cousin who inherits massive wealth and has never learned to handle money, or the drug addict chasing that next high – the money and the rush are soon gone as are all the trappings which accompanied them. I have walked into that scenario several times in poker games going from "zero to hero" and then descending to a quick walk from the table. Winning big hands and accumulating a massive stack are fantastic feelings, a great rush and the buzz we all chase. But often on the tail of that rush comes the desire to relive it – immediately. So with a big stack at our disposal we begin betting at any given opportunity. We stop playing the game we were playing that allowed us to gain such a big advantage and unwittingly squander all the gains we have made. We become temporarily drunk on the chips (or power) we have gained and it goes to our heads. The mindset is usually such that as soon as we start losing we begin

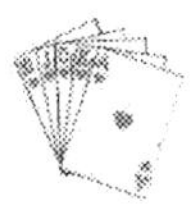

taking more and more risks in a vain attempt to get back what we have lost. Next thing you know, you guessed it, the game is over.

As far as dealing with this situation is concerned, and you will all experience it at some stage in your playing career, a simple strategy is all that is needed to avoid making this mistake. For example, I might make a point of not playing all but my top 6 hands for the next two rounds so that I can regain my composure and get back to playing the strategy that brought me to this point. It is really up to you how you decide to deal with this issue. The main point here is that you need to have a plan in place that is ready to be implemented the moment you find yourself, or realise, you might be getting a little "chip drunk".

2. Be Aware of Your Play. Another situation you also need to be mindful of is slowing your play down, or tightening up, too much. I have been guilty of this and it is a very unnerving feeling when you realise that the gain you had in the not too distant past has been whittled away because you have not taken the action you should have. In order to combat that issue I try to keep in mind, (along with a thousand other factors) what the blinds are what the average stack size is and are there any time constraints? Appling some simple strategies, having a plan, and being focussed will help you to avoid these types of pitfalls.

SMALL CHIP STACK

A small stack size is obviously not a position you want to find yourself in. Although it clearly applies pressure as to how you play, there are a couple of small advantages you can utilise as being the "short stack" at the table.

Advantages:

1. You will come across players who cannot help but attack the short stacked players. They may be the table bully or a mid-stack that is simply in a hurry to build their chips. You can often take advantage of this and strike with mediocre starting hands noting that there is a very good possibility that your opponent is playing less than average hands in an effort to push you out. In many

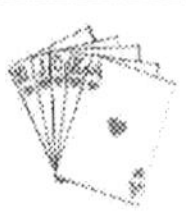

tournaments I have recovered to go on to win from positions that looked beyond desperate purely because other players wanted to get rid of the short stack.

2. Another slight advantage of being short stacked (some may disagree) is that you are basically forced to take more risks because of the predicament you find yourself in. Given that poker does contain an element of luck "the coin toss" is an even money opportunity that can bring you fortune. It is a situation that I generally try to avoid however as a short stack sometimes throwing caution to the wind can reap rewards.

Element 4: Table Position

Table position is another aspect of the game that all players need to gain an understanding of. "Position" has a great impact on how you play, when you play and what strategies you employ during play. Your table position in Texas Hold'em is determined by where you are sitting in relation to the dealer and is described as falling into one of three groups. Early Position, Mid-Position and Late Position.

Position is important because it dictates the relative strength of your hand in relation to other players and the reason for this is because your position dictates when you can act. Think of it this way - one of the main skills in poker is "information gathering". The more information you have, the better prepared you are for the inevitable decision. Bet, call, raise or fold. When you are in a position that allows you to see what all of the other players are doing before you have to act, gives you have a powerful advantage. So it is when you sit on the button in the dealer position as all players except the blinds have to act before you pre-flop.

Let's just have a quick look at a scenario to illustrate the point. I am sitting to the left of the big blind and therefore I am the first to act pre-flop. I have an A-10 off suit. As we have studied our charts, we know that this particular starting hand is ranked 42 and not an overly strong hand - certainly not one that I would class as of my "A" hands. Given that I am the first to act it is fair to assume that some of the players to follow have far stronger hands. Based on very little information from the other players at this point, I am faced with a dilemma - what should I do?

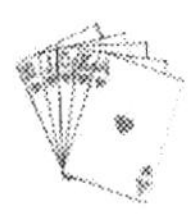

Now let's take the same hand except this time I am sitting in the dealer position. I am now able to observe everyone's actions (except the blinds) before it is my turn to act. I think you will agree that the information I now possess changes the "relative" strength of my hand. In my original position, I face the possibility of eight players producing any of the 41 better hands that I hold. However, if everyone folds to the button where I am now stationed with the same hand, I now only have two other players to consider (the blinds) and both of those players have been forced to bet.

Diagram 7 – Positions (9 Player Table)

POSITION	PLAYERS
Early Position	Small Blind (SB); Big Blind (BB); Player 3
Mid Position	Player 4; Player 5; Player 6
Late Position	Player 7; Player 8; Dealer (D)

For the moment let us familiarise ourselves with a few more terms and take a closer look at the positions we find around our nine-player poker table.

Diagram 8 – Position Terms

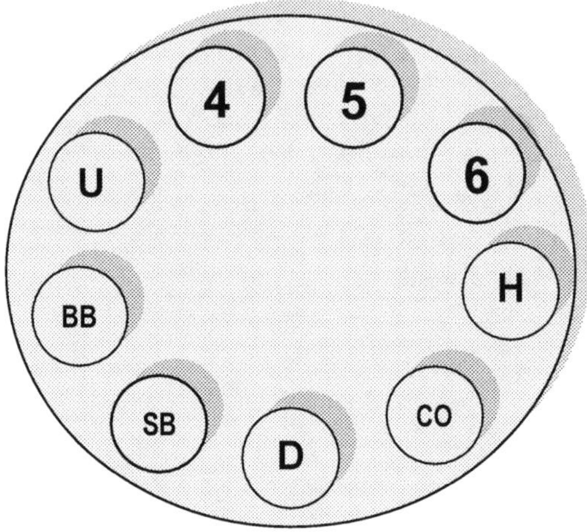

EARLY POSITIONS

Small Blind (SB) – the first position to the left of the dealer and is required to post, in most cases, half the minimum bet. The small blind is the first of the three early positions and the first to be dealt cards during a round.

Big Blind (BB) – the second position to the left of the dealer and is required to post the minimum bet. The big blind is the last to act pre-flop and by virtue of this fact has an advantage which can be utilised at this stage of the game.

Player 3 - Under the Gun (U). The final early position on our nine-player table. It is considered by most to be the worst and the hardest position to play because the pressure is on this player to act first. The U player does not have the benefit of seeing how other players are going to act therefore, the amount of information he receives is severely limited.

MID POSITIONS

Players 4, 5 and 6 are considered mid positions. The advantage is greater as we move clockwise due to the previous players' actions and making their decisions known.

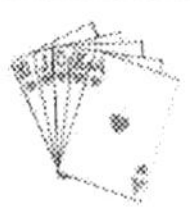

LATE POSITIONS

The last three positions on a table are considered to be late positions. One of the benefits of being in these positions is the power to "steal" the blinds. Stealing blinds is yet another strategy used by players to build up chip stacks by taking advantage of the fact that the blinds are forced bets. This is another aspect of the game that you must develop through further reading and studying.

Player 7 – Hijack (H). The H player is the first position that is considered to be a late position and the advantage here is that this player can "hijack" the next player's attempt to steal the blinds. This player also has the added advantage of having seen how the previous four players acted.

Player 8 - Cut Off (CO). Again this position refers to the stealing of blinds and is so named because of the player's ability to "cut-off" the Dealer's attempt to steal the blinds. In addition to being able to utilise this strategy, this player has the added advantage of having seen the actions of the five previous players.

Dealer (D) - otherwise known as "the button". The Dealer is responsible for dealing the cards or, in the case where a dealer is provided, the button is representative of that player dealing. The dealer is in the strongest position at any table because he is in the most powerful position in relation to stealing the blinds. He has the added advantage of having seen all players' actions except for those of the blinds.

Research Question 6

How fast can Chris Ferguson
throw a playing card?

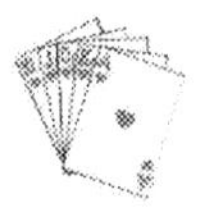

Element 5: Starting Hands to Play

Now that we have spent some time coming to grips with the hand ranks, stack size and table position, we now find ourselves dealing with the million dollar question.

What hands should I play and when?

In Lesson 12 I am going to be offering several small book reviews with the intention of providing you with your next step toward taking your game to the level you wish to achieve. My starting hands and the way I play evolves at a varied rate. Some days I don't feel I have learned anything, some days I think I have regressed and other days I feel I have taken my understanding of the game to an entirely new level. This is one of the main reasons I continue to be drawn to poker.

There are many (and often conflicted) opinions as to which hands should be played and when. Over time I have memorised the "recommended" best starting hands in an effort to improve my game. At the end of the book I provide links to websites that will help you develop your game including your starting hands. For the moment I will share with you how I, for the most part, approach the beginning of each hand.

A large amount of information needs to be processed before a player acts. What I am about to describe is an extremely good place to begin developing your game. As a rule, I play my game following a basic script that has been drawn from countless hours playing, numerous websites visited, frequent late night TV games watched, and many books read. It is the culmination of all things "poker" that has brought me to this point.

Please note - It is up to you to develop your own style and you will only achieve this by "paying your dues" with time in games, heads in books and conversations with those people who love poker as much as you do.

The following diagram is an indication of the hands I play from each position pre-flop, provided no one else has raised. In other words I must be the first person to act. I adopted this as a starting point in my game and have drawn this directly from the Starting Hand Guide produced by professional poker player, Mike Caro.

Mike Caro, aka "the mad genius of poker", is extremely well known and well respected in the poker community. Not only for his poker prowess, books and website, but it has also been said that he has trained more poker players than anyone else. His website www.poker1.com is a must for all players.

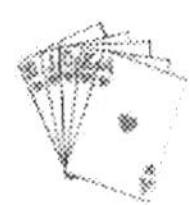

Diagram 9 – Starting Hands (9 Player table)

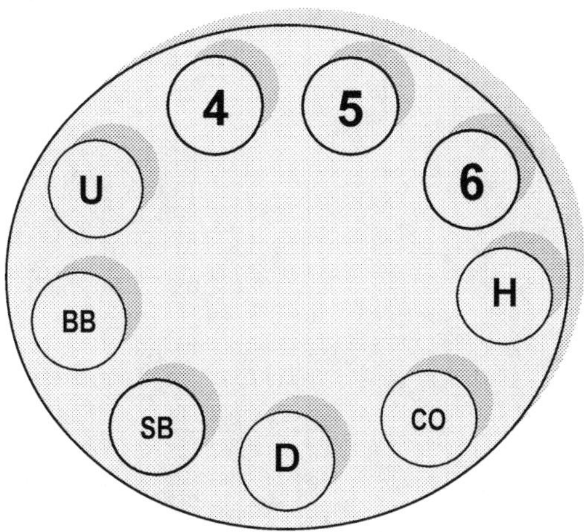

Position	Starting Hands
U	A-A; K-K; Q-Q; J-J; A-Ks; A-Ko; A-Qs; A-Js
4	The above plus - A-Qo; A-10s; 10-10
5	All of the above plus - A-Jo; K-Qs; 9-9
6	All of the above plus - A-10o; K-Qo; K-Js; Q-Js; J-10s; 10-9s; 8-8
H	All of the above plus - A-9o; A-(Any suited kicker); K-Jo; 7-7
CO	All of the above plus - A-(8-7-6o); K-(10-9o); Q-(J-10); K-(10-9-8s); Q-(10-9s); J-9s; 6-6
D	All of the above plus - A-(5-4-3-2o); K-(8-7-6o); Q-(9-8o); J-(10-9o); 10-9o; K-(7-6-5-4-3-2s); Q-(8-7-6-5s); J-(8-7s); 10-(8-7s); 9-(8-7s); 8-7s; 5-5; 4-4

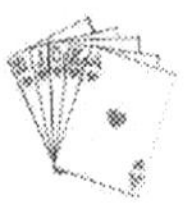

Explanation:

The purpose of this diagram is to provide you with a solid starting point for your game, something to build on with regard to your own game plan and strategy. This is a great table to memorise and once you have committed it to memory you will find that the decision making process becomes a little easier.

When positioned Under the Gun (U), the only hands you should play are those indicated. (A-A; K-K; Q-Q; J-J; A-Ks; A-Ko; A-Qs; A-Js).

As you move to a different position with each new hand dealt, add the previous group of starting hands to your current ones. For example:- If you are in Position 4 you would play the starting hand for 4 as well as those for U. (A-A; K-K; Q-Q; J-J; A-Ks; A-Ko; A-Qs; A-Js & A-Qo; A-10s; 10-10).

Continue to add playable hands as your position changes. For example:- If you are in the Cut Off (CO) position you would play all the starting hands listed for U, 4, 5, 6, H and CO.

Important Note: I need to emphasise that the table only deals with the cards you should play when you are the FIRST to act!!! That is – any preceding players have folded and the blinds have not been called or raised. How much to bet; whether you call or fold if raised; are all part of the style and strategy that you are going to develop over time.

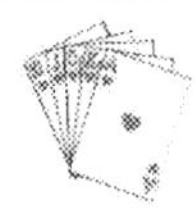

LESSON 7 - GAME MANAGEMENT

The longer you're not taking action
the more money you're losing.

Carrie Wilkerson
(Executive, Women's mentor / coach / advisor)

Learning Outcomes

In Lesson 7 we will learn about the importance of bankroll management and tracking results.

Element 1: Bankroll Management

1.1 Cash Game Bankroll

1.2 Tournament Bankroll

Element 2: Tracking Results

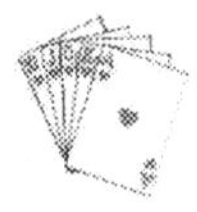

Element 1: Bankroll Management

Having a good grasp of bankroll management is extremely important for new and experienced poker players alike and is one of the keys to becoming a successful poker player.

"Fear is an affirmation of your growth because it proves that you are risking."

Rhonda Britten – (Actress and Author)

FEAR!! It is only through experience, practice, and commitment that we are able to build confidence and with confidence we eliminate or reduce our fear of failure. Fear is good in healthy doses and I know that when I play at levels or buy-ins that are beyond my bankroll requirements, the fear factor increases.

By and large, the result is that I stop playing my "own" game and begin making mistakes. While we are playing at our correct level and sticking to our bankroll requirements we reduce the fear factor because we are not jeopardising more than we can afford to lose. The result is that we reduce the pressure we are placing on ourselves. Generally speaking, when we play at the correct level we are also going to be playing against people of a similar skill level. This also helps to settle to the nerves and help us to focus on our own game.

In order to manage a bankroll the first major decision we need to make is - How much money do we have to invest in our poker game? Now I hear you ask – invest?

I treat my poker game and all things associated with it as an investment. Like buying shares or investing in real estate, we need to know how much we can afford to spend and what are the types of resources we are going to require to become successful. Poker is no different. In order for you to become successful, you are going to be required to spend time studying, buying books, surfing the internet, maybe some travel and of course, paying for games.

My approach is to first work out how much money I can afford to invest / spend in a year. I like to use a calendar year, some players may prefer a

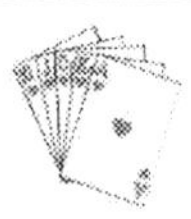

financial year - this is really a personal choice. Once we have ascertained how much money we can put into our "hobby", we then need to formulate a budget.

The annual poker budget is a key process required to maintain your strategy while ensuring you don't exceed your financial limitations. Furthermore, it provides discipline, gives you direction and helps you set achievable goals, again without breaking the bank.

For you to be successful when setting your budget you need to identify the areas where you wish to spend money. I have prepared a sample budget just to give you an idea. This does not need to be complicated, we are just putting a simple plan in place that will help us better manage our game and finances.

Diagram 10 – Example Budget

2012 Poker Budget		
Resource	**Unit Cost**	**Yearly Total**
Books	6 ea @ $25	$150
DVD's	6 ea @ $25	$150
Magazine Subscriptions	2 ea @ $75	$150
Apparel	Chip guards, Cards, T-shirts	$260
Computer Software	2 Programs	$230
On-line games	$20 Per Week	$1,040
Home Games	$10 Per Week	$520
Travel / Accom		$1,500
Total		**$4,000**

Once we have established our budget for the year, we will now be able to calculate an annual "bankroll". I view my bankroll as being a specific figure relating to how much money I have to spend playing poker (paying for games).

As can be seen from the example budget, I have allocated $1,040 for on-line games and $520 for home games giving me a total allocation of $1,560 for my bankroll. Regardless of the types of games I may be going to play, this is my starting figure for that year. The moment I begin playing my bankroll figure will change. Higher or lower, depending on whether I am winning or losing. It is this movement that is going to determine which games I can and can't play for the remainder of the year according to affordability. I will explain this in a little more detail as the lesson progresses.

As can be seen in the example budget, it is envisioned that I will spend money on all sorts of poker-related resources in addition to putting money into my games. I have to admit that I tend not to track my "other poker stuff" spending as well as I should, basically because if I can afford to buy a poker related product – I do. At this stage in my playing career, I do not require such an amount for travel but I have included it as it is something we should consider depending on where our poker playing career takes us.

Tracking your poker bankroll (the actual amount of money set aside for playing games) is an entirely different issue. This should be monitored and adhered to with strict and constant discipline. I can't see myself going broke buying one too many T-shirts or packs of cards but I can certainly foresee that possibility without having a good system to manage my bankroll.

We must also accept that our budget is an evolving tool. By this I mean as our hobby grows, so does the list of resources we require to fully expand on our interest. As such, we need to cater for these changes. (I have decided to travel to Melbourne to play in the Aussie Millions; clearly some big adjustments need to be made to my budget.)

Remember, your budget and money management processes are tools that you will use to manage your future.

Now is your chance to think about what you plan to spend money on and create your first simple poker budget using the following diagram provided.

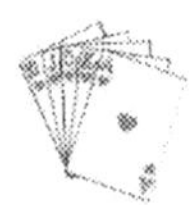

Diagram 11 – Personal Budget

Poker Budget		
Resource	**Unit Cost**	**Yearly Total**
Total		**$**

1.1 Cash Game Bankroll

The cash game bankroll is based on 100 big blind buy-ins. As I have previously stated, it is our intention to get into any cash game with the maximum permissible buy-in. That being said, we also do not want to risk more than 5% of our total bankroll at any given time.

Use the following table to guide you when making decisions as to which cash games you should be playing.

Diagram 12 – Cash Game Bankroll Guide

Cash Game Bankroll Guide			
SB	**BB**	**Buy-In (100xBB)**	**Bankroll**
1c	2c	$2	$40
2c	4c	$4	$80
5c	10c	$10	$200
10c	20c	$20	$400
25c	50c	$50	$1,000
50c	$1	$100	$2,000
$1	$2	$200	$4,000
$2	$4	$400	$8,000
$5	$10	$1,000	$20,000
$10	$20	$2,000	$40,000
$25	$50	$5,000	$100,000
$50	$100	$10,000	$200,000
$100	$200	$20,000	$400,000
$250	$500	$50,000	$1,000,000

For example, in a cash game with a small blind of 1c and a big blind of 2c, we would take $2 into the game and only if we have a minimum total bankroll of $40. (100 big blinds of 2c = $2; $2 = 5% of our total bankroll of $40.)

Given that this blind structure is about the smallest you will come across, I would suggest that if you can't afford to lose $40 over a one-year period then you should reconsider playing cash games of any description and just remain with "play money".

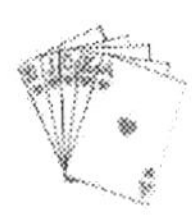

1.2 Tournament Bankroll

The tournament bankroll is based on 40 games of a specific tournament buy-in. For example, if we have a bankroll of $120 the most we can pay for a tournament buy-in is $3. Once again this is the maximum buy-in we can play with our allotted bankroll and obviously, if we play at lower buy-in levels we are able to play more games.

Use the following diagram to guide you when making decisions as to which tournament games you should be playing.

Diagram 13 – Tournament Bankroll Guide

Tournament Bankroll Guide	
Tournament Buy-in	Bankroll
10c	$4
$1	$40
$2	$80
$3	$120
$4	$160
$5	$200
$6	$240
$10	$400
$12	$480
$16	$640
$20	$800
$25	$1,000
$50	$2,000
$100	$4,000

I have added these Bankroll Guides as a good starting point based on my research and how I mange my own bankroll. Every player has a different style and some players may require a higher bankroll for the buy-ins, while others may not, depending upon how they play.

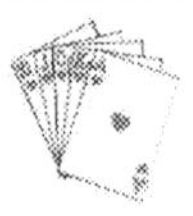

The main point to note here is:-

*You **MUST** have a bankroll and*
adhere to the rules you have set for yourself.

WHAT IS MY BUDGET?	
WHAT IS MY BANKROLL?	

Once we have established our bankroll we can now work out the type of games we wish to play and the frequency that we wish to play them.

Let us assume that for a moment that I have a bankroll of $4,000. This means that if I wish to play cash games only then the maximum blind structure I can play is a $1 / $2 game (100 big blinds of $2 = $200; $200 = 5% of bankroll of $4,000). It also means that I will be able to play 20 games in a year at this level $200 x 20 = $4,000).

This of course assumes that I am going to lose each and every game. Clearly, I am not planning to lose all my money each game I play but this is the worst case scenario. Based on this information I can now work out how often I will play. As can be seen I need to spread the 20 games I wish to play over the course of the year.

The fact of the matter is that we are not going to play in this manner, especially when we are just starting out. We are going to want to try all sorts of formats and experiment with various types of games. After all, how else are we going to find the games that work for us if not by being adventurous and experimenting. The entire point of the bankroll is to give us our 'upper limit" of play so that, as I have said, we do not go broke.

In Element 2 of this lesson I will be providing you with some strategies I use to maintain my bankroll as well as ensuring that I am still having fun while incorporating challenges that help me to develop my game.

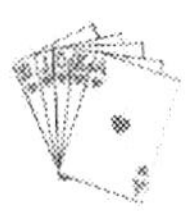

Using our $4,000 example we can also see that if I wish to play tournaments only then the highest buy-in tournament I can play in is $100 (40 games x $100 = $4,000). As such, I simply need to work out where and when I wish to play my tournaments for the year.

The same logic applies for tournaments as it does for cash games. In the real world of poker, I will be playing a range of tournaments in an effort to find those that are enjoyable and profitable for me.

In summary, as your bankroll increases you can move your game to higher buy-in levels. Consequently, as your bankroll decreases you must drop your range accordingly.

What do we do if we use all our bankroll?

- Keep playing - use play money only;
- Read, watch the games on TV and study;
- Do anything else that involves learning more about your game and why your bankroll has been depleted.

But no matter the temptation, you must not put more money into playing. Exercise some discipline and patience and wait until it is time for you to work out your next annual budget and bankroll, and then start playing at the level which is appropriate.

Research Question 7

What are the following players' nicknames:
Mike Caro, Paul Magriel,
Howard Lederer and Robert Williamson?

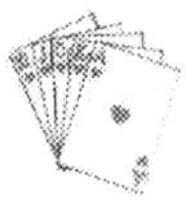

Element 2: Tracking Results

The truth about where you stand in relation to your wins and losses will only be as good as the records you keep. We all remember the big wins but try to put the losses behind us. We all like to talk about the big games but quite often seem a little shy when it comes to discussing the hits we have taken. Our minds begin to play tricks on us and before we know it we believe we are a consistent winner and this is when we begin to dig a hole for ourselves with regard to our own finances.

Poker is about discipline on so many levels. Not least of which is the discipline required to accurately and honestly record the results we have been achieving.

There are several reasons why it is extremely important that you track the results your games. Tracking results using data that is specific, relevant and current provides us with information on how to:-

a. Better manage our finances through the highs and lows of poker so that we do not go broke playing.

b. Identify the games that are profitable to us and the games we should be avoiding.

c. Identify the strengths and weaknesses in our game. For example: Am I a better tournament player or better at cash games? Do I like longer games or prefer short sessions (Am I patient or impatient)?

d. Reduce the amount of pressure on our game because we are playing within our means and to a financial script.

Above all, the reason we track game results is so that we can aim for continuous improvement. The monitoring or tracking process is essential, because changes in our performance occur as our game evolves. It is only through tracking results that we can establish what is working and what is not and then take corrective action where and when needed.

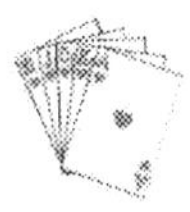

In order to monitor our playing performance we need to follow four basic steps:-

1. **Set Goals**

   While progressing through the Getting Started section of this book we established some SMART goals and detailed some of the issues we may be confronted with. Now it is time to refer back to this section and refresh your memories. What is your main goal?

2. **Play and Monitor Progress**

   Start playing, stick to our levels and track results on our own tracking sheets according to the information we have chosen to include.

3. **Review and Assess**

   Using our tracking sheets, we will now be able to review the data and very quickly get a feel for what is working and what is not.

4. **Reassess and Adjust**

   Based upon our observations when reviewing our results we can make a range of decisions that will help to improve our game.

In order for the previous four points to have any meaning we really have to examine our tracking sheet. I have an included example of a tracking sheet as well as included a similar template at the end of this lesson.
I now use tracking software but until you have spent some time playing, I would suggest using a spreadsheet. It is a cheap and effective way of tracking your games.

The tracking sheet I used in 2009 was a bit more involved than the template I have included in this book and was created using Microsoft Excel to assist in the calculations.

Following is a breakdown of the sections that I used in this tracking sheet. It will provide you with the type of information I would suggest you use to record your game results.

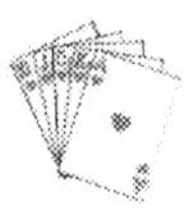

2009 Poker Tracking Sheets

1. **Heading** - Simple and straight forward - because I know I will be tracking results yearly.

Monthly Target $300 / $10 per day		
In the Money	Final Table	No Finish

TOTAL ANNUAL PAYOUT	$341.75
MONTHLY PAYOUT TOTAL	$104.80

2. **Monthly Target** - In this case you can see that my monthly target was $300 which I then broke down to $10 per day. So my main goal for 2009 was to increase my bankroll by $3,600.

3. **Shading** - In the money, final tables, no finish. Shading these games as such gives me a quick reference as I look through each sheet. It makes it very easy to identify trends. For example, if I have a series of games where I have finished in the money they will stand out, as will the type of game it is. Very quickly I can see what I games I should be playing.

4. **Total Annual Payout** – As can be seen my total annual payout to this point was $ 341.75. This is important because it allows me very quickly to see how I am tracking for the year.

5. **Monthly Payout Total** – My total monthly payout to this point was $ 104.80 and is important because it allows me very quickly to see how I am tracking for that month.

Monthly Information	
Monthly Target to Date	-$195.20
Total Buy-In Invested	$468.70
Total Payout Received	$573.50
No. Games Played Month	145
No. Games Played Year	516
Average Placing	5
Average Payout	$3.98
Opening Balance	-$33.00

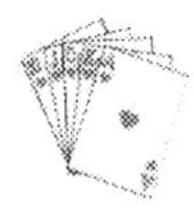

Total Profit / Loss	$71.80
Payout Percentage	58.82%

My monthly information section is a summation of several key pieces of information I require to analyse correctly where I stand at any given moment of play.

6. **Monthly Target to Date –** A simple calculation, my monthly target minus my current monthly winnings.

7. **Total Buy-in Invested –** How much money I have paid to play games.

8. **Total Payout Received –** How much money I have received playing those games.

9. **No. Games Played Month –** The number of games I have played for that particular month. A very useful inclusion as I can check from year to year which months are historically profitable and then look for reasons why.

10. **No. Games Played Year –** Games I have played in total for the year. Handy for future reference. Bear in mind that for me poker is something I will be enjoying for the remainder of my days.

11. **Average Placing –** This is another extremely useful section when used in conjunction with a filter. For example in MS Excel I can apply a filter for the year that allows me to look at all the $5 – 45-man tournaments I have played in. Then look at average placing and make decisions with regards to those games.

12. **Average Payout -** The same advantage as Average Placing except I can work out my return on investment and this better equips me to decide which games I will be playing in the future.

13. **Opening Balance –** This figure is carried over from the previous months balance. A quick reference as to how well I did in the previous month (not very well in this case!).

14. **Total Profit / Loss –** My total profit loss for the month. Monthly Payout Total minus Opening Balance.

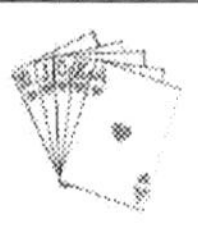

15. Payout Percentage - Another very helpful piece of information as this accurately reflects the percentage of games I have received payouts for during the month.

Game	Date	Game Type	Buy-in
1	1	10 Man Double up	$10.40
2	1	10 Man Double up	$10.40
3	1	10 Man Double up	$10.40
4	2	10 Man Double up	$10.40
5	2	180 Man Turbo	$2.20
6	2	180 Man Turbo	$2.20
7	2	2 Man Heads Up	$2.20
8	3	9 Man Turbo	$6.50
9	4	10 Man Double up	$10.40
10	4	2 Man Heads Up	$2.20

16. Game – Included for no other reason except as a quick reference to how many games I have played that month.

17. Date – Tracking dates may seem like a waste of time but this is a good form of subtle feedback you are hoping to gain from your tracking sheets. Let's say I notice a trend, I seem to be regularly losing a few games every seven days. Closer analysis shows me this is occurring every Friday night and I am playing a lot of games. Now that I have found a common trend in my losses I can now look to why. End of the week and I am tired? Distracted with family or other issues? Once you discover a trend finding the cause becomes so much easier and a solution will naturally follow.

18. Game Type – EXTREMELY IMPORTANT!! Game type has to be tracked and no matter what else you choose to include or exclude in your tracking method, you must include this reference. Without knowing the type of games you are playing you will not be able to make any sound decisions as to what you should or should not be playing. Your progression depends on it.

19. Buy-in – As with game type, you need to know which levels are profitable and which are not, so it is vital that we include this information. In addition, we also want to know what sort of return we are going to get with a win or a place. Some games give you a higher return than others, such as tournaments. Clearly the games we are looking to find are those with a good return on our

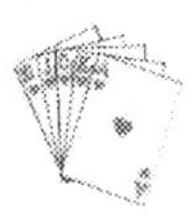

money when we win, as well as games that we will be winning more often than not. We can see in the example that I actually do quite well in the 10-Man Double up - $10.40 games. These are games where 10 players start and the top 5 players win and you will note that we just fall short of doubling our money when winning these games.

Position	Payout	Balance	Time in Play
1	$20.00	$9.60	43
1	$20.00	$9.60	35
1	$20.00	$9.60	34
8	$0.00	-$10.40	23
76	$0.00	-$2.20	22
43	$0.00	-$2.20	23
1	$4.00	$1.80	18
4	$0.00	-$6.50	45
6	$0.00	-$10.40	32
1	$4.00	$1.80	32

20. **Position** – Without knowing where I finished all other information becomes irrelevant.

21. **Payout** – How much I received for the position I finished in.

22. **Balance** – Like all investments, we need to know what we are earning, where from and when we are earning it. The importance of this is self-explanatory. Balance represents the winnings minus the cost to enter the tournament.

23. **Time in Play** – This is very helpful when determining which tournaments you want to play for a number of reasons. The obvious reason, it is nice to know that I have a spare two hours and can get 2 games in based on the information I have collected. As we progress and move up levels we will no longer be satisfied winning a certain amount per hour, we are going to want to increase that. In the same way we began working, for most of us it was at the bottom and the pay was representative of that fact. As we gained more experience and got better at our jobs we expected to be rewarded accordingly. Well poker is much the same, as you get better you will expect the rewards to be greater, and they will. (Still have not quit my day job but I am working on

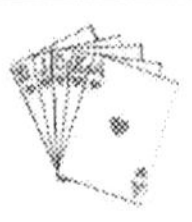

it). The time we spend playing particular tournaments is important because as they say, time is money.

Comments
Good Patient play again 6th win straight
Hard slog, made a couple of blunders - in a rush
Again quite good won a big hand that could have hurt - QQ
Slow played the high ace again and it cost me.
Played the wrong hands sat on the ones I should have played.
Played like cr@p!!
Steady again
What a load of cr@p!! - guy called with nothing & hit the river
Got impatient when it counted.
Steady again

24. Comments - This is going to be your main source of feedback and in the example I have given you I don't think I have done this very well. "cr@p" really does not provide feedback that is useful. In short, we want information that is going to help us in future games.

When providing feedback for your own use your comments should be:-

a. **Specific –** Address as many issues as you can cover in shortest way possible without compromising the value of the information.

b. **Relevant -** Keep your comments relevant and not personal. These sheets are about recording facts not emotions.

c. **Timely –** Put your comments in as soon as you finish a game don't try to add comments later in the day or the following several games. Your information will not be accurate.

Examples of the type of feedback I place in my sheets:-

- Tired, distracted, lost - all-in QQ from small blind while short stacked. Not aggressive enough after break, (last 20 min). Impatient.

- Focussed, played to the plan & remained aggressive throughout. Avoided 2 all-in calls with KA & JJ. Lost heads up, (HU) all-in 5,5 BB - GG

The information provided in your comments section taken with the other information on your sheets such as time in play and type of game will provide you with an excellent resource for analysing your game.

Now I appreciate that this section may have been a little hard to digest for some readers. My only hope is that you take away the point that tracking results is vital and it is really one of the main tools you require that will allow you to improve your game. At the very least start by using the tracking template sheet I have provided. A little bit of time spent at the end of every game filling in your sheets will return dividends in no time.

A final note - There is a vast range of poker software available that allows you to do everything from tracking games results hand by hand, to identifying holes or leaks in your game. My personal feeling is that you should develop your game and manual tracking skills before you start investing in these other programs but that point is certainly debatable.

Tracking Sheet Example

In the example following you can see that I made up my own codes for game information so that I do not have to input a lot of data. Once you begin playing you can make up your own.

BRD .... Bankroll to date

BI/S .... Buy-in / Stake in $

9PC .... Nine-player cash game

HG15P .... Home game 15-players

Pos .... Position finished

PO .... Payout in $

TIP .... Time In Play in minutes

Bal .... Balance, money made

6PT .... Six-player turbo tournament

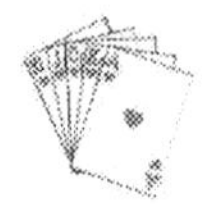

Diagram 14 – Example Tracking Sheet Guide

TRACKING SHEET - OCTOBER 2012						
BRD	$ 2,500.00		**DATE:**		7 October 2012	
No	**Game Type**	**BI / S**	**Pos**	**PO**	**TIP**	**Bal**
1	6PT	$10	2	$40	45	+ $35
Comments: Good Game, Lost Heads Up all-in J,10s. Played to plan. Relaxed						
2	HG15P	$20	4	$60	320	+ $40
Comments:						
3	9PC	$18	0	$0	30	- $18
Comments:						
4						
Comments:						
5						
Comments:						

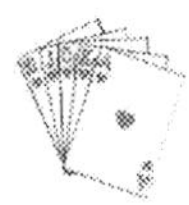

Diagram 15 – Personal Tracking Sheet

TRACKING SHEET						
BRD	$		DATE:			
No	Game Type	BI / S	Pos	PO	TIP	Bal
1						
Comments:						
2						
Comments:						
3						
Comments:						
4						
Comments:						
5						
Comments:						

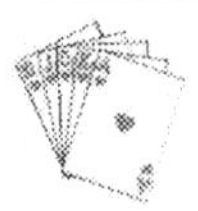

LESSON 8 - HOME GAMES & PRACTICE EXERCISES

"Knowing is not enough; we must apply.
Willing is not enough; we must do."

Wolfgang Goethe
(German writer artist and politician)

Learning Outcomes

In Lesson 8 I will be providing you with a few more terms as well as introducing you to several practice exercises that will help you to develop your game without costing you an arm and a leg. We then run through the process of establishing your own home game.

Element 1: Terms to Get Us Started

Element 2: On-line Games

Element 3: Home Games

3.1 Establishing a Home Game

3.2 Home Game Structure

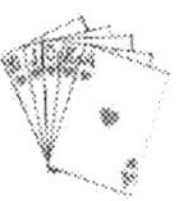

Element 1: Terms to Get Us Started

Aggressive - An aggressive player is one who is involved in a lot of hands and usually bets or raises.

Crack - To beat. “He cracked Aces” he won against a pair of aces.

Dead - A player's hand that cannot be played.

Loose - A player who plays many hands, often inferior.

Multi-table – A player who plays more than one table or game at a time.

Re-buys - an option to buy back into a tournament after you've lost all your chips.

Satellite - A tournament where the prize is a free entrance to another (larger) tournament.

Stake - The amount a player buys in for and can bet.

Street - The name applied to each phase of play. For example, the river is often called fourth street.

Tell - An action or comment that gives away information about one's cards.

Tight - A player who rarely calls.

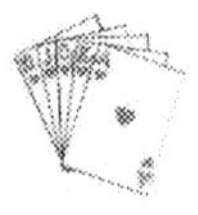

Element 2: On-line Games

There are many sites that you can join with varying levels for beginners and a range of joining bonuses, each with a variety of functionality and appeal. The two sites I use for my on-line poker are *www.pokerstars.com* and *www.888poker.com.au*. Personally I like the functionality and the range of games associated with both sites and it is for these reasons that I stick with them.

Real money or play money? That is the question. It is fantastic that so many sites offer the ability to play poker using play money instead of real cash. Play money simply means you are not playing for real money whether you are playing in tournaments or cash games. This offers players the ability to learn the game, experiment and venture out into a range of other games without jeopardising their finances. Transitioning from play money to real money is certainly a personal choice and one that should not be taken lightly. Money management and game tracking, as previously discussed, are the two main methods of ensuring that you play within your means.

Practice game strategy.

When I find I am getting into a rut or not playing to the best of my ability over a period of time then I impose upon myself a "punishment" of sorts. I stop playing higher stake real money games and revert back to lower stakes or play money. I find that if I do this occasionally, it grounds my game and I can get back to playing the way I should. For the most part I try to play a tight and aggressive game. In other words I pick my hands carefully and bet heavily. I find that if I stray too much from this strategy then reverting back to play money or lower stake cash games helps me to get my game back on track.

I must stress at this point - You are going to develop your own style of play and it will evolve - as does my style of play. I am playing at the correct levels and really enjoying myself and when the time is right I will move up. The reason I developed these exercises and others like it, was so that I had a method of "getting my head back in the game". I do find they help the mental and emotional aspects of my game enormously.

Enter *www.pokerstars.com* or *www.pokerstars.net*, then go to Hold'em / Play Money / $5/$10 and follow the directions provided.

PLAY MONEY CHALLENGES

Challenge 1 - Million Dollar Challenge

When we join either *pokerstars.com* or *pokerstars.net* we are given a starting stack of $1,000 play money. In both of these sites you are allowed several re-loads (re-buys), so this means you can start playing very loose and aggressive because you really have nothing to lose. The Million Dollar Challenge, as I call it, is about taking your original starting stack of $1,000 and turning it into $1 million as quickly as possible. Money management is not really an issue here as we are not playing for real stakes. Just go for it and re-load when you get knocked out. The real discipline does not begin until you have begun building your bankroll.

The following guide is aimed at giving you direction as to how to build your stack. REMEMBER – This is Play Money!! Enter *www.pokerstars.com* or *www.pokerstars.net*, then go to Hold'em / Play Money / $5/$10 and follow the directions provided.

Cash $5/$10

- Aggressive loose play, until I have achieved more than $5,000, then I move to next stage. I try to double up on each hand I play given that you recieve several re-loads.

Cash $25/$50

- My play remains similar with the aim of achieving more than $12,000, then I move to next stage. Although still playing loose / aggressive I do tighten up a little and wait for better opportunities.

Cash $100/$200

- Now change play and become a little more selective with starting hands. Remain aggressive and your new target is more than $100,000. Once there move to next stage.

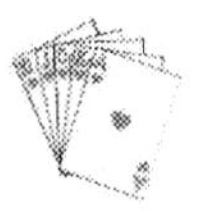

Once I have achieved more than $100,000 I move from play money cash games into play money tournaments. This is where you can approach this part of the challenge in several different ways. You can either play single tables and build your stack or begin to multi-table. I suggest as a beginner you should stick to one table at a time however, if you want to try multi-tables then just try two until you get used to it.

My personal preferences are nine-player tournaments as they go a little quicker and prize money is distributed to the top three players. I like to play multi-table with four games when playing the $25,000 buy-in but as I said, just play one or two tables to start with.

Tourney $25,000

- Aggressive tight play, until I have achieved more than $250,000, then I move to next stage. I now really focus on playing my game and sticking to my plan while playing at this level.

Tourney $50,000

- My play remains similar with the aim of achieving more than $500,000, then I move to next stage. I play aggressive and tight but if I am multi-tabling I only play 2 tables.

Tourney $100,000

- I continue with the same stategy as previously with $1 million now the target. If my bankroll drops below the previous target (in this case $500,000), then I move back one level.

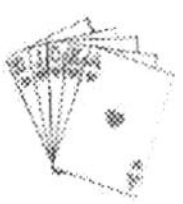

Challenge 2 - Triple Play (Cash Game)

Generally speaking most of the poker players who make money do so from cash games. I recently read that it was estimated that professional poker players playing tournaments on average make the money 1 in 9 and on average actually win 1 in 30. The money to fund these tournaments is made playing cash games.

Clearly this is a very broad statement and will vary from person to person but speaking for myself I can say that cash games absolutely fund my tournaments and keep my account moving forward.

The challenge I am about to outline is directly related to money management and is a very good way to practice your bankroll discipline. This is another method of slowing down your loss rate while giving you the opportunity to increase your bankroll. A little bit of insurance if you like.

For example:-

We have $90 left available to play with according to our bankroll guidelines (cash game = 5% of $1800). In the Triple Play Challenge this means that we will now enter a game with a maximum buy-in of $30 ($90 divided by 3). As soon as we win and increase our minimum balance we can move up a level. However if we lose our total of $90, then we can play again or revert back to standard bankroll guidelines. This will ensure that you keep playing for quite some time.

Yes it may become a little frustrating but in the end you will not go broke and you will learn to discipline yourself as far as your bankroll is concerned.

I have included a table to help work out when and what to play. No cheating!! As soon as you finish a session and find you have dropped below your minimum balance then you must go down to the next level.

Research Question 8

How much money did Stu Ungar have to his name when he was found dead in 1998?

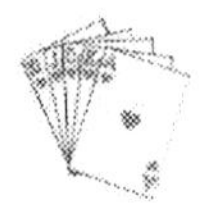

Diagram 16 – Triple Play Guide.

Min Balance	Blind	Buy-in
$6	1c / 2c	$2
$30	5c / 10c	$10
$60	10c / 20c	$20
$150	25c / 50c	$50
$300	50c / $1	$100
$600	$1 / $2	$200
$1,500	$2 / $5	$500
$3,000	$5 / $10	$1,000

REAL MONEY CHALLENGES

Challenge 1 – Tournament Challenge

I have put together a couple of different types of challenges for real money cash tournaments but my "Track and Move" is extremely useful in gauging your level and then providing direction as to which games you should be playing next.

Create a small spreadsheet with the base information included as shown in the table provided. Build your table in the manner shown in the previous chapter.

Diagram 17 – Track and Move Guide.

No. Of Players	Entry Fee $			
2 (heads up)	1 - 4	5 - 10	11 - 20	21 -50
6	1 - 4	5 - 10	11 - 20	21 -50
9	1 - 4	5 - 10	11 - 20	21 -50
18	1 - 4	5 - 10	11 - 20	21 -50
27	1 - 4	5 - 10	11 - 20	21 -50
45	1 - 4	5 - 10	11 - 20	21 -50
90	1 - 4	5 - 10	11 - 20	21 -50
180	1 - 4	5 - 10	11 - 20	21 -50

The aim of this challenge is to discover which games you enjoy and which are profitable. Each game should be played twenty times so when you build your spread sheet ensure you consider this.

The process is as follows:-

1. Select the game (number of players and the entry fee). For example, 6-player table at $2.20 (this entry fee falls in the $1 - $4 range). Remember, we still need to be following money management guidelines.

2. Play this format 20 times recording your results, ensuring that you review each game and try to identify weaknesses or strengths.

3. If, at the end of 20 games, you find that you have finished in profit then move to the next entry fee bracket ($5 - $10). Remain with the 6-player games.

4. When you have played 20 games at this level and you do not finish in profit then stop playing this level. Record the last profitable level then move to the next stage, i.e. 9-player table at $1 - $4 entry fee and repeat the process.

5. If you are playing at the lowest level and have not finished in profit after 20 games either try again or resume normal play. You do not want to get frustrated with this process, it is about gathering

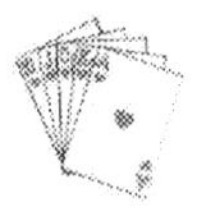

information. If you begin to get impatient with the process you will stop being objective and your results will not provide you with accurate feedback.

6. Once you have played and finished profitable on each game (6 to 180 players) then you will have a very good indication of which games you can now play with a good likelihood of making money. This also gives you a guide as to which games are going to provide a challenge for you. It is the challenging games that you will have to start playing later in order to improve your game.

Challenge 2 – Weekly 3 x Stakes

Find a tournament that is three times the player size and entry fee you would normally play in (so long as this does not contradict normal bankroll guidelines).

For example, if you are playing quite a few 9-player games with an entry fee is $5 then find a game that is about $15 to play with at least 27 players. This is not a formula that needs to be set in stone. The point is to get you playing in tournaments that are out of your normal comfort zone and allow you to experience some different types of games while expanding on your own ability to find games that work for you.

Challenge 3 – Monthly High Stake

This is a personal favourite. Once a month I like to enter a big tournament of several thousand people paying a higher buy-in than I would normally would. In addition, I will always try to win a ticket into these higher stake tournaments by playing satellites. In the event that I am not successful in the satellite games, I will pay the fee (grin and bear it) and try my luck.

NOTE:- With each of these challenges it is important that we do not exceed our maximum buy-ins in proportion to our bankroll requirements.

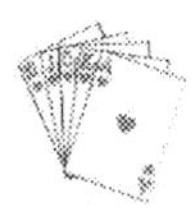

Element 3: Home Games

3.1 Establishing a Home Game

Establishing your own home game is a wonderfully fulfilling and exciting pursuit. Not only will it bring your friends closer together but it will allow you to hone your own skills in an environment of your own making or choosing. The home game will help to improve your game and I believe it is an important part in learning to play poker properly. If you can't find a local group to join then creating your own is the next best thing. To help you with this, Element 3 is designed to provide you everything you will require to establish a successful home game.

Establishment of a home game allows you to:-

(a) Practice honing your poker skills and experiment with different strategies while consolidating your knowledge about the game.

(b) Practice identifying tells, not only in the friends you are playing with but also in yourself. When you identify tells in other players it is important that you keep this information to yourself to be used to your advantage when required. However "Trade-a-Tell" is a fun way to liven up conversation and the game if you are playing in a friendly atmosphere.

(c) Build a network of friends with a common interest.

(d) Develop some personal traits and skills. Improve personal character traits such as patience or management abilities.

TOURNAMENT DIRECTOR

If you have decided to create your own home game then you have taken on the responsibility of becoming the leader for your group. You are the tournament director for a group of friends with a common interest and as such it is vital that you follow a few basic tenants of leadership. I will say this, leadership will not always be an easy task and can at times be quite a personal challenge.

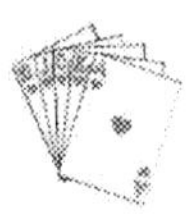

Dealing with a variety of personalities and opinions will test your resolve. If you want your game to survive you must rise above these issues and keep in mind your goal – to run a fair and fun game. Some of you may be great leaders, some of you may not be. That being said, the following are a few points which will help you better manage your group and game:-

1. **Self-Improvement –** Spend some time trying to improve any defects of character. Working on yourself will help you become a better leader. It will help you to develop your strengths and eliminate or reduce the effects of your weaknesses.

2. **Develop Your Technical Proficiency –** Read, write, learn. Immerse yourself in all things poker (that doesn't necessarily mean become fanatical). Develop your skills surrounding the game, its players and your understanding of the rules. In the next chapter we will be looking at the "PEA" principle, and it is this principle which will give you the tools to further advance your game and technical ability.

3. **Take Responsibility** - Search for ways to keep the group interested and engaged. When things go wrong, don't blame others and don't get into arguments or debates. Simply analyse the situation, take corrective action, and move on to the next challenge.

4. **Make Sound and Timely Decisions** – Ensure you make decisions honestly and openly and be willing to admit it when that you don't have an answer. Acknowledge the opinions and input of others and use their strengths to further improve the functionality of the group and enjoyment of the game.

5. **Set the Example** - Be a good role model and lead in a manner that is respectful, knowledgeable and inspiring. Now I have to admit that I have had my moments and failed on occasion in this department. It is important to realise that we are all flawed human beings and occasionally make mistakes. Be willing to correct those mistakes and apologise where and when necessary. An acknowledgment of you own failings will gain you respect. Stubborn denial (a big river in Egypt) of the things you have done wrong, won't!!

6. **Communication** - I have a simple and firm belief that most issues in life revolve around communication. To be a good leader you need to communicate with your group clearly and effectively so you can achieve the group's needs or goals. I generally find this can be achieved in one of two ways. At the beginning of each game I will address the group and ask the players to table any issues and then as a group we will discuss them. I also distribute a newsletter to the group the week following the game outlining any issues discussed and providing a summary of the previous game's play.

7. **Assign Tasks / Responsibility** – You may need to delegate tasks within your group to maintain your own sanity but an easier way is simply ask for help. You will find that for the most part the majority of people will want to contribute to maintaining a successful group.

8. **Treat Your Group as a Team** – Run an inclusive group that allows all to contribute equally. Some of your group may be a little more out spoken than others. Try to calm the waters and lead the group to a positive outcome. This can be a fine balancing act but the rewards make it all worthwhile and a velvet glove rather than an iron fist will help you to achieve this.

Research Question 9

Why is Antonio Esfandiari called "the Magician"?

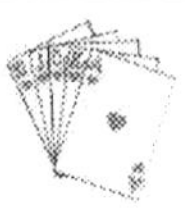

GAME CONSIDERATIONS

Over the course of three years our home group grew and contracted. One aspect of how we functioned was that we always discussed any issues that were raised in the previous game and looked toward possible solutions. We would then vote on the solution we thought may best suit us all. In order to function efficiently and effectively it is necessary to establish some "house rules". Although these will change as your group grows and matures they will remain essential to ensuring your game, survives. This should keep things challenging, exciting and fun.

Below is a list of some considerations and basic house rules and that you might want to implement or consider for your own group:-

1. **Group Size –** It has been my experience that you really do not want your group to grow much beyond 18 players. For ten or more players we separate evenly onto two tables and then join as one as soon as the remaining players have reduced to eight. Generally I have found trying to run three tables becomes quite difficult to manage and as such I recommend that you aim for a home game group of between ten and twenty.

2. **Seating Position –** Seating position does become more important once you have been playing together for a while. Some players find it easy to steal blinds off others and so it is important that with every game you have a system that caters for this issue. We originally just drew cards for the tables and each player who drew a black card would be on one table while each player who drew a red card would be on the other. This random approach worked for a while however as the game expanded we then decided to put together a spread sheet and rotate each player so that they were assured of a different seating position each game. Although a little effort was required to ensure that this worked well, it did prove to be effective and fair while keeping the game light and fun. We are also playing for prize money so it is important that we run a game that is as fair as possible for all players.

3. **Points and Prize Structure –** One of the really great ways to encourage your players to keep attending is to introduce a points and prizes structure for the year. This will encourage competition as well as provide incentives for your players to improve their games. Once again there are many ways you can manage this but simplicity is the key.

If for example we have sixteen players turn up for a game then sixteen points is up for grabs. The winner would receive sixteen points with the person getting knocked out first getting one point. I tried several different ways to run a points system but found this method to be the fairest and easiest to manage. Of course the points system requires a reward and as such we introduced a system of prizes for not only each game but also for the year. I will discuss payouts for the game at the end of this section but as far as prizes for the year are concerned, we have several:-

(a) Champion – Player who finishes on top of the ladder.

(b) Placings – Second and Third.

(c) Best and Fairest – The player who finishes high on the points board but was also considered to be the fairest player as voted by all the other players.

(d) Outstanding Player – This is awarded to the player who wins the most games in the year. This does not necessarily represent the player who had the most points in the year.

(e) Most Improved – The player who shows the most improved finishes throughout the year.

(f) Rising Star – This is an encouragement award.

(g) Wooden Spoon – A prize, usually something comical awarded to the player who finished last on the points board.

With each game we also had two trophies that could be taken home and held by players until the next game. One for the player who won the game and another for the person who had the biggest "dummy spit" (who got the most upset). I took that one home a few times!! The dummy spit award is fantastic because it allows people to feel free to express their frustrations without feeling that they are going to be ejected from the group for being a little bad tempered. Poker players can get very emotional and copping the trophy is a great way to keep the game fun.

Initially we awarded trophies for each of the awards but at the end of the second year the group decided that practical prizes would

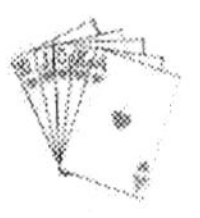

represent money better spent. So we did away with the trophies and introduced prizes such as, dinner for two, poker chip sets or simply cash.

Last but not least, we also had a prize we all called the "chocolate frog". When a player knocked out the winner from the previous game, they were instantly awarded a bag of chocolate frogs, which generally everyone got to enjoy anyway.

4. **Game Frequency** – Definitely a case of Goldilocks and the Three Bears. We experimented with varying periods between games and after a bit of trial and error we found that a three week cycle worked very well. Players at the three week mark were just starting to itch for a game and our participation rate remained high. We tried a game every two weeks and the general feeling was that life interfered too much and the number of attendees tended to drop, (the porridge was just way too hot). A month gap was too big and what we found was that people were starting to host interim games because they wanted a poker fix, (the porridge was way too cold). A three week cycle gives you approximately 16 games for the year and keeps everyone keen and keen is what we hope to maintain. (Mmmm, the porridge was just right).

5. **Accepting New Players** – Our group began with myself and two other friends, (Hello to Ken and Scotty) at work and on our lunch break. I had been watching poker on TV the previous few weeks and was keen to learn to play. As it happened Scotty was a bit of poker fanatic and took the time to teach me the basics during lunch time sessions. As you do when you discover something that you enjoy, you talk to your other friends, and very quickly I found that a couple of them already knew how to play. From there our home group was born.

   Our first game had seven players, most complete novices, except Scotty who remained patient as we all learned the ropes. It turned out to be very exciting as well as being a fantastic night with friends. Over the next year our group rose to a membership of about 16 regular players, with our biggest game getting an attendance of 22. This meant running three tables which did not work particularly well.

   Now there were two reasons why we came together as a group. Firstly, to play poker and learn to play better poker. Secondly, as a social get-together, a good excuse for a group of friends to meet and catch up. Our group developed its own culture and we all felt happy

with each other's company and level of poker. No one player was really any better than the next and this made for a great competition every time we came together.

In order to build the group we invited friends to play and obviously if they enjoyed it would become a part of the game on a regular basis. Unfortunately we became a victim of our own popularity and we started to get players coming to our group who were not there for the same reasons we were. Some of our guests simply wanted to take money off the learners, some wanted to treat the game as an excuse to get drunk and some, well, I have no idea why they bothered to show up! In short, these players began to affect the feeling and the attitude within the group. As such, we decided to leave the invitations open only to those players who respected the group and our game. We were able to maintain the type of game we all wanted and although a few egos may have been hurt, generally the approach was successful.

6. **Social / Serious play –** I play with some other friends who come together primarily to play poker. They are not coming together for the social aspect of the game instead they want to play some serious poker. On the other hand I play with a group whose main priority is a "good reason to catch up" Establishing the type of game you want to play in is important and will save you a lot of heart ache if you make your reason for playing clear from the start.

7. **Game Rotation –** It was also decided among group members that games would be hosted at a different venue. Players were asked if they would like to host a game and a roster was created. It was great playing at different homes and added variety as well as letting the players contribute to the group.

Research Question 10

How many one-eyed Jacks are there in a deck of cards?
What suits are they?

HOUSE RULES

Every home game should have its own set of "house" rules as they will simplify explanations, clarify expectations, and create a fair and enjoyable environment for your players. The following ideas are meant as a guide to the type of rules you may want to consider for your game:-

1. **Cost** – Establish a base cost for your games. We decided that for our tournament structure a $20 entry fee was paid with an additional $5 contribution for food. We also made our cash game blinds 10c/20c with a maximum buy-in of $20 per night. The reason we used $20 as a base figure is because we did not want the game getting too serious and very quickly where money is concerned, this can happen. We also wanted the players who won to walk away with a reasonable payout for the night's effort.

2. **Game Play** – Keeping the game flowing while accommodating the needs of those wishing to get a drink, go to the toilet or have a smoke can be a balancing act. We found the easiest way to deal with this was to make a rule that if a player is not at the table when it is their turn to act then their hand is automatically folded. Allowing players to tell the player following them in the action to fold their cards when it was their turn was another way we managed to keep the flow of the game going while giving the players a quick break.

3. **Table Talk** – By table talk, I mean discussing the hand possibilities once the flop, turn or river has hit the table. "Oh no, that is ugly open-ended straight possibility." I believe allowing table talk is a vital part of the learning process in a beginner's game and should be encouraged. This helps players to identify hands and become familiar with the possibilities as the cards change with each street. It also helps to foster a friendly game. Another type of table talk is showing other players your dead cards before a hand has finished. This can give those players who are still in the hand vital information about the hand in play. Showing each other your cards that are still in play should not be allowed under any circumstances. Discuss what cards you had after the hand has been completed.

4. **Misdeal** – You will need to clearly define what constitutes a misdeal. For example if a card is exposed during the deal or if a person does not receive both cards. Generally we left the call of a misdeal up to the discretion of the dealer but on occasion a decision would be left to majority vote by the players at the table if the dealer was unsure.

5. **Behaviour** - I have discussed etiquette in the previous chapter. As a tournament director and friend to the players you have a responsibility to ensure that an acceptable level of behaviour is maintained. There will be times when you need to address issues but generally you are going to be playing with friends and as such the level of etiquette required will go unspoken.

6. **Electronic Gadgets** – Although we tried to foster a relaxed atmosphere around our games the issue of mobile phones in particular became one of contention. Easy solution - if you need to use the phone then do it away from the game and your hand will be folded if you are not present when it is your turn. Take this stance and save yourself a headache from the start.

7. **Rabbit Hunting** - (checking out the next card; e.g. the turn or river card after the flop assuming everyone folds). This is a practice that is frowned upon in some groups however our players generally accepted it as part of the game. Personally I think you are just asking to torture yourself not to mention giving away information about your hand and the hands you do or don't play. In the spirit of fun we all felt that this practise was not really an issue.

8. **Late Arrivals** – You are always going to experience people arriving late and in order to maintain the flow of the game I asked all players to call if they were going to be late. There are definitely a few different ways you can manage late arrivals but what we found to work the best was to assume that all the regulars would be playing and post blinds for those absent. (Hands are then automatically folded each round). In our tournament structure the cut off for joining the game was at the end of the dinner break. If a person had not shown up by this stage or not called then it would be assumed that they would not be attending and their remaining stack would be removed from the table.

9. **Bankers** – As Tournament Director, at the start of every game I collect the money from each player then conduct a quick check to ensure that I have the collected the correct amount. There is nothing worse than getting left short of cash at the end of a nights play because you have not accounted for the funds correctly. I also place all the starting stacks and check to see that they are correct. We as a group assigned one person to carry out the chip changes and issue of extra chips. It is important that we run an honest and fair game and as such

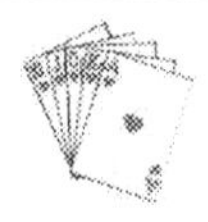

giving one trusted member of your group the role of chip changer ensures that confusion and suspicion of inappropriate behaviour does not occur.

10. **Dealer Rotation –** When players are eliminated this can often interrupt the position of the dealer and blinds. In other words I may now find myself having to deal when I was actually not due to deal for another hand or so. There are a couple of different ways to manage this however to save a lot of confusion it was our experience that simple was best. As such it is my recommendation that you simply move the dealer button to the next position and continue play as you would under normal playing circumstances.

    Following is an example of how we dealt with the elimination of the blinds.

Diagram 18 – Dealer Rotation

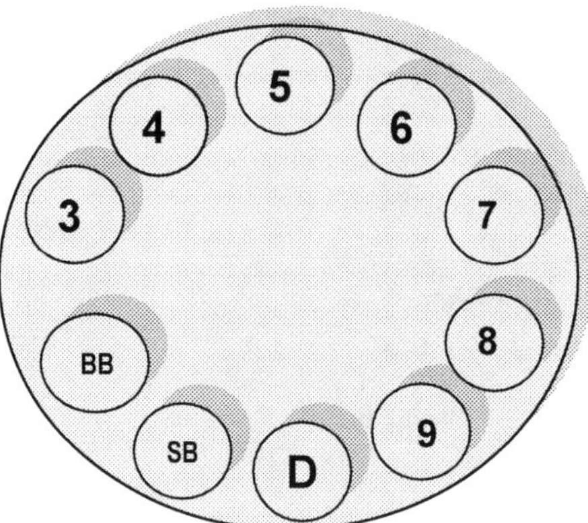

Example 1 – Let's assume that this is the table position at a given hand. The cards have been dealt, the hand played and the small blind has been eliminated. The dealer button on the next deal moves to the big blind position, bypassing the eliminated small blind. The new small blind is now at position 3 and the big blind moves to position 4.

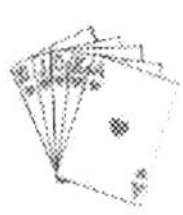

Example 2 – Same table position at a given hand, cards have been dealt, hand played and both the small blind and position 3 have been eliminated. The dealer button on the next deal moves to the big blind position, bypassing the eliminated small blind as in Example 1. However, because position 3 has also been eliminated, the new small blind now goes to position 4 with position 5 becoming the big blind.

11. **Balancing tables** – (For games with more than one starting table). Keeping an even number of players (or as close as possible) on your tables is vital. This ensures that a similar number of hands are played during a level as well as maintaining an equal playing field in relation to the number of competitors each player is competing against.

    As the game progresses players get eliminated and it is your job as tournament director to control the game ensuring the tables remain as balanced as possible. When a player is knocked out take a quick check of numbers and if the number of players on one table is two or more than the other table then you need to announce that play is to be halted on both tables at the end of each tables hand. The table that has the greater number of players on it must then lose a player/s to the table with the lesser number. The player/s who is required to move will be the player who sat directly to the right of the dealer during the last hand played. They will then move to the same position on the opposite table.

    In the previous Diagram 18 you will note that player 9 will be the player moving and being seated in the equivalent seat on the receiving table. If in the event that two players need to be moved then they will be moved from and seated in the next position, i.e. seat 8.

SOCIAL PLAY

In an effort to keep the game interesting we also introduced several fun aspects into the night in the way of chip bonuses:-

1. **The Nutcracker – A-A ($500).** Awarded to any player who cracks aces. If a player holds AA and plays the hand out to showdown then loses, the winning player is awarded the prize.

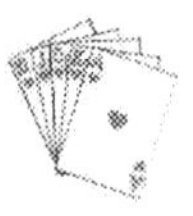

2. **Bounty Hunter – ($1,000).** Awarded to the player who knocks out the player who won the previous tournament. In addition the player who achieved this was also given a bag of chocolate frogs.

3. **Bluff – ($500).** On the example blind structure chart outlined in Diagram 19, you will note the inclusion of "bluff hands". If a player plays and wins a hand at a particular level with the hand required then the bonus is awarded. For example in the 25/50 blind you can see that the bluff hand is 4,9 off suit. Win with that hand and you are receive the chip bonus.

4. **First Deal Bonus – ($250).** There are several ways to decide who deals initially but really just keep it simple, deal cards to each player face up - first jack is the dealer. This bonus is awarded to the initial dealer on each of the tables.

5. **Pair – ($500).** You will note that following the dinner break each blind has a pair attached to it. If a player wins with one of these hands then they receive the bonus.

The sky is the limit as far as inventing ways to keep your game entertaining and enjoyable. Ask your group for suggestions then give them a go. If it doesn't work then try something else. Trial and error really is the key to a successful home game but what I have done here is to provide you with a very good starting point.

Research Question 11

To make any straight, there are one of two cards required.

What are these two cards?

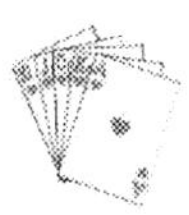

OUR GAME

You will need to invest a small amount of money getting set up. There are a multitude of websites that you can use to find all the equipment and information you want but I would suggest that a great place to start is *www.homepokertourney.com*. This site offers extensive information on setting up your home game as well providing numerous links to a variety of tools, accessories and other poker sites.

So - what do we need?

Of course the most important thing we need is Players!!

Other than players you are going to require several other items if you want your home game to run smoothly.

1. **Chips** - Given that we are aiming to establish a group of around 20 players a thousand piece poker set is preferable. The type of set you need to purchase that may best suit your needs could contain 5, 10, 25, 50, 100, 500 and 1000 denomination chips.

2. **Cards** - You will obviously need cards and basically you can go one of two ways here. Buy either very good quality plastic cards that will last you quite a few games or alternatively, cheap paper cards that you will replace at the start of each game. Plastic cards can be expensive so my choice was to buy bulk paper cards and at the start of each game we would play with a new pack of cards. It is very important that you do not play with cards that have been marked as observant players will note these cards and this clearly gives an unfair advantage to those players.

3. **Timers** - You will also need to buy a least one timer, so that you can keep track of the blinds. Given that we were routinely separated onto two tables, we found that it was better having two timers and nominating a timekeeper on each table. I tried to run one timer but it very quickly became an annoyance, because I had to constantly remind the other table when the blinds had gone up. Synchronise timers and let each table manage themselves - more time for you to enjoy the game. While we are on the subject of timers, there are a lot of products out there and we tried several. In the end cheap, battery-operated egg timers from the local supermarket worked just as well as anything else.

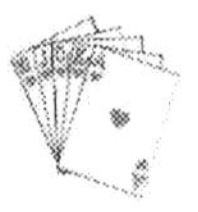

4. **Tables and Chairs** – This can be an area you find yourself wanting to spend quite a bit of money but my advice is, don't do it to start with. (Maybe later when you get a little more established.) As with most things poker there is a huge variety of options but cheap, portable tables and chairs did the trick for our group. Fold up rectangular tables that can comfortably sit eight people can get ten players around them if you need to and they work fine.

   One of our group members made a poker table with cup holders and a felt surface which was fantastic, while another group member bought a real one. I know we all looked forward to playing at their homes so we could play on the "good" tables. But given that our games were played at various homes, we needed tables and chairs that were functional and portable. Besides, nice poker orientated table cloths go a long way to change the look of your cheaper tables.

3.2 Home Game Structure

Diagram 19 is an example of how we set up our own home game and came about through a lot of trial, error, discussion and debate. In the end we produced a game that for the most part met everyone's needs - no mean feat. This home game structure was developed for a group ranging between 6 and 23 players and given that our core group size was 16 players, this structure worked very well.

This game has been set up to run for approximately six to seven hours depending upon the number of players. Because of the group's differing commitments, it was decided that all games would be played on Saturday with a start time of 3.00pm. Finding a balance between your start and finish time is very important. You do not want the game running too late, especially if you have players with children in the group. By the same token, you also want the game to be an enjoyable and great night's entertainment and not finish too soon.

STARTING STACK

In our group, each player is issued 4,500 in chips broken down into the following denominations:-

8 x 25; 10 x 50; 8 x 100; 4 x 500; and 1 x 1,000

Diagram 19 - Blind Structure & Bonus Hands

Round	Blinds (SB / BB)	Bonus
1	25 / 50	4 -9os
2	50 / 100	2 - 6os
3	75 / 150	3 - 7os
4	100 / 200	3 - 8os
5	150 / 300	2 - 8os
6	200 / 400	2 - 7os
7	250 / 500	2 - 10os
	First Break	
8	300 / 600	2 - 2
9	400 / 800	3 - 3
10	500 / 1,000	4 - 4
11	600 / 1,200	5 - 5
12	800 / 1,600	6 - 6
13	1,000 / 2,000	7 - 7
	Second Break	
14	1,500 / 3,000	None
15	2,000 / 4,000	None
16	2,500 / 5,000	None
17	3,000 / 6,000	None
18	4,000 / 8,000	None
19	5,000 / 10,000	None
20	6,000 / 12,000	None
21	7,000 / 14,000	None
22	8,000 / 16,000	None
23	9,000 / 18,000	None
24	10,000 / 20,000	None

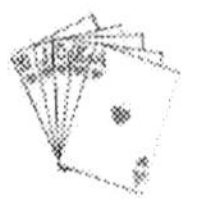

TIMING

Rounds 1 – 7 are 20 minute blinds giving us 2½ hours of play before the first break. Given the start time of 3.00pm this means our first break occurs at 6.00pm – just in time for dinner!!

We generally aim for no more than a one hour break at this stage. That provides enough time for everyone to eat, have a stretch and be itching to get back into the game. We also take the opportunity during the break to change out the chips and get rid of all the 25 and 50 chips which are no longer necessary.

Following the first break, we now move into 15 minute blinds for Rounds 8 - 13. You will notice that the first blinds following the break are 300 / 600. Prior to starting play, every player including those eliminated before the break, are given another 1,800 in chips. We give each player this amount so that those players who were knocked out before the break are re-joining the game with enough chips to play two full rounds. This then gives them the chance to possibly double up and get back into the game.

Once we have finished Round 13, we take another break. This one is shorter, just long enough to conduct another chip change, have a stretch and quick chat. At this stage of the game we also cease the Bonus hands.

Rounds 14 – 24 are then played at ten minute blind intervals until all but one player have been eliminated.

PRIZE MONEY DISTRIBUTION

Our home game had a $20 entry fee or stake per player. Once the buy-ins were collected, we kept $30 from the takings and put this money in our "kitty" or "fund". This money is put towards prizes and awards as well as the general running of the club for purchases such as new cards, chocolate frogs or replacement chips.

Diagram 20 has been provided as a guide to prize money distribution. How the prize pool would be divided among the winners was the subject of huge debate. Some players wanted more positions paid while others wanted less. This diagram is the result of a lot of compromise and I believe it works very well.

Example 1:-

For 6 players we see $90 for the prize pool. (6 players x $20 = $120 less $30 for the kitty.) Prize money is given to first and second, $60 and $30 respectively.

Example 2:-

For 17 players there would be $310 for the prize pool. (17 players x $20 = $340 less $30 for the kitty.) Prize money is paid to the players in first to sixth place in the amounts of $130, $70, $50, $30, $20 and $10 respectively.

Diagram 20 – Prize Money Distribution

Players	Prize Pool	Distribution
6	$90	$60, $30
7	$110	$60, $30, $20
8	$130	$70, $40, $20
9	$150	$80, $50, $20
10	$170	$90, $50, $20, $10
11	$190	$100, $60, $20, $10
12	$210	$110, $60, $30, $10
13	$230	$110, $60, $30, $20, $10
14	$250	$120, $60, $40, $20, $10
15	$270	$120, $70, $40, $30, $10
16	$290	$130, $70, $40, $30, $20
17	$310	$130, $70, $50, $30, $20, $10
18	$330	$140, $80, $50, $30, $20, $10
19	$350	$140, $80, $60, $40, $20, $10
20	$370	$150, $80, $60, $40, $30, $10
21	$390	$150, $90, $60, $40, $30, $20
22	$410	$160, $90, $60, $40, $30, $20, $10
23	$430	$160, $90, $70, $40, $30, $20, $10

TOURNAMENT WITH RE-BUY FORMAT

Occasionally we would organise impromptu games and play slightly different formats to our normal tournament game. One of the formats that we used was designed as a tournament with a re-buy and a bit of a cash game twist.

The game is structured in the following manner:-

1. Time in play is set prior to game commencing. In other words, we start and finish at specific times. Generally this was a six- hour game with a break for dinner. Each round lasted for one hour and we also used a blind format so as to keep the momentum of the game moving.

Diagram 21 – Blind Structure

Duration	Round	Blinds
1 hour	1	5 / 10
1 hour	2	10 / 20
1 hour	3	20 / 40
Dinner Break		
1 hour	4	25 / 50
1 hour	5	50 / 100
1 hour +	6	100 / 200

2. Players may join the game at any stage after the start time and no penalties are imposed.

3. All starting players pay $10 to receive their initial buy-in of 1,000 in chips. Chips are issued in the following denominations:- 6 x 5; 12 x 10; 12 x 25; and 11 x 50.

4. As new players arrive to join the game or any of the original starting players re-buy, then the prize pool increases accordingly. I have provided a Payout Structure in Diagram 22 so that you can easily track the buy-ins / re-buys. I just use the sheet and place a cross over the number that corresponds.

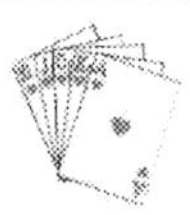

For example, say six players begin the game so cross out the number 6 in the Buy-ins column. Shortly afterward, a new player arrives and another decides to re-buy so you would cross out the numbers 7 & 8 to account for these. You would continue on in this fashion for any new arrivals or re-buys.

5. For every $10 buy-in or re-buy collected, $1 from each is put toward the two bonuses. The balance then goes toward the prize pool. In this game, the bonus payouts are based on two hands only. "American Airlines" (A-A) beat the player with the aces and you win, and "The Hammer" (7-2os) win with this hand and the bonus is yours. Let's continue with the above example where we started out with six players, had a new arrival and a re-buy. This means we have now collected 8 buy-ins and $8 toward our bonuses. As we have two bonuses per game the payout would $4 per bonus at this stage. In the event that the bonuses have already been claimed and players have continued to re-buy then I simply add the bonus component to first prize. This is also the case should the bonuses not be awarded for the duration of the game.

6. Tables must remain as balanced as possible. Occasionally players would only do an initial buy-in and once knocked out, they would leave. This coupled with players arriving late means you have to closely monitor the table numbers as you would in any other tournament.

7. Two re-buys of $10 (1000 in chips each) are permitted but only after each of the previous stacks of 1,000 amounts have been expended. This limits the total night's cost per person to $30. As with the Home Game Tournament structure, we did not want the games becoming too serious or too high stake. If a player uses both re-buys and loses all their chips then they are eliminated from the game.

8. The game ends when either all but one player have been eliminated or the finish time is reached. Once the remaining players are reduced to four then the prize money will be distributed as each player is knocked out. In the event that the several players are still playing then when the time limit is reached then prizes will be allocated according to chip stack size. With this tournament or any other tournament that uses a time based structure it is vital that you watch the clock and plan your strategies accordingly.

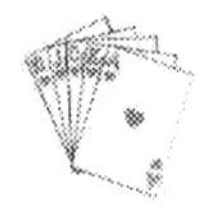

Diagram 22 – Payout Structure

Buy-ins	Prize Pool	Prize Payout 1ST	2ND	3RD	4TH	Bonus Payout
6	$54	$32	$14	$7	$1	$3
7	$63	$37	$16	$8	$2	$3.50
8	$72	$42	$18	$9	$3	$4
9	$81	$47	$20	$10	$4	$4.50
10	$90	$52	$22	$11	$5	$5
11	$99	$57	$24	$12	$6	$5.50
12	$108	$62	$26	$13	$7	$6
13	$117	$67	$28	$14	$8	$6.50
14	$126	$72	$30	$15	$9	$7
15	$135	$77	$32	$16	$10	$7.50
16	$144	$83	$34	$17	$10	$8
17	$153	$89	$36	$18	$10	$8.50
18	$162	$95	$38	$19	$10	$9
19	$171	$101	$40	$20	$10	$9.50
20	$180	$105	$42	$21	$12	$10
21	$189	$111	$44	$22	$12	$10.50
22	$198	$117	$46	$23	$12	$11
23	$207	$123	$48	$24	$12	$11.50
24	$216	$129	$50	$25	$12	$12

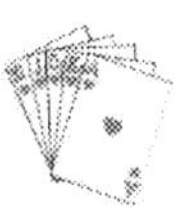

LESSON 9 - THE "PEA" PRINCIPLE

"Success doesn't come to you, you go to it."

Marva Collins
(American educator)

Learning Outcomes

In Lesson 9 we will examine the PEA principle. The PEA principle relates to what I believe are the three fundamental requirements needed to achieve success, in whatever field or endeavour you chose to pursue - *Perseverance, Education* and *Association.*

The purpose of this lesson is not to turn you into goal-setting experts or achievement-driven individuals. Rather the aim here is to simply provide you with another basic tool which will allow you to improve your game.

Element 1: Perseverance

Element 2: Education

Element 3: Association

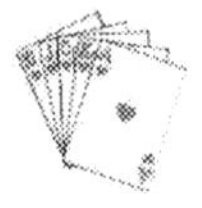

The reasons why the PEA principle works for me:-

PERSEVERANCE:

Success in my life has clearly been achieved when I have followed this basic principle whether knowingly or not. My wife and I have been together for over 20 years - why?

Beside that fact that we are still in love, it has been because we have persevered when times were difficult. We communicated; focussed on the reasons we wanted to be together and worked through any issues together. In short – we stuck it out.

EDUCATION:

We also took the time to educate ourselves. We learned about relationships, marriage, raising children and a multitude of other areas by way of books, on-line forums and DVD's. We continue to do these things in good times and bad because the process of learning should never cease.

Circumstances change, people change, environments change, but the key is to continually adapt through education and the result will be – "success".

ASSOCIATION:

Finally, we associated with people who also had successful relationships. We took lessons from them and applied these to our own situations. When you spend time with people who are successful in their relationships, careers or life interests their accomplishments and triumphs will rub off on you.

Our financial and business successes have been driven following exactly the same principle while repeating the basic methods that have been tried and proven. When something works for you, keep repeating it. In the following lesson I will expand on each of the three elements that encompass the PEA principle. It is my hope that you take the points raised here and apply them to your game.

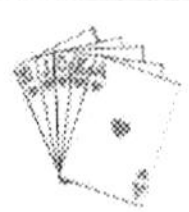

Element 1: Perseverance

"We are made to persist.
That's how we find out who we are."

Tobias Wolff -
(Soldier, professor and writer)

In order for us to become successful poker players we must remain flexible yet dedicated to our purpose or goal, i.e. play within our bankroll requirements and adjust the type of game we are playing in order to keep increasing profit. We must also explore and challenge the ideas or biases we have in relation to the outcomes we hope to achieve, so that we do not become discouraged and ultimately fail. For example, I have often heard people, who generally don't play poker, comment that the game is simply about luck. Do you have a preconceived notion about luck and poker? Does this affect how you play?

Perseverance is much more than doggedly sticking to our purpose. Like so many other aspects of poker, perseverance requires discipline, direction and focus. In order to remain committed and resolute we need to be able to set performance standards, measure those standards, compare our performance to bench marks, analyse results and then take corrective action. This all sounds very complicated but in actuality it really isn't. In fact, you have already taken the initial steps to achieve this. Bankroll management and tracking your results are the two main tools you will now be using to stay committed or persevere.

Setting performance standards simply means playing at our correct level, exercising a little patience when becoming frustrated at those levels, or accepting that sometimes we will need to drop back a level in order to take on board a few more vital lessons. The process I am about to highlight will not be unfamiliar to you. I have no doubt that most, if not all of the people reading this, will have gone through this process on more than one occasion. We all have to deal with problems and find solutions in life. I would now like to discuss this process in the context of poker.

Diagram 23 – The Problem Solving Cycle

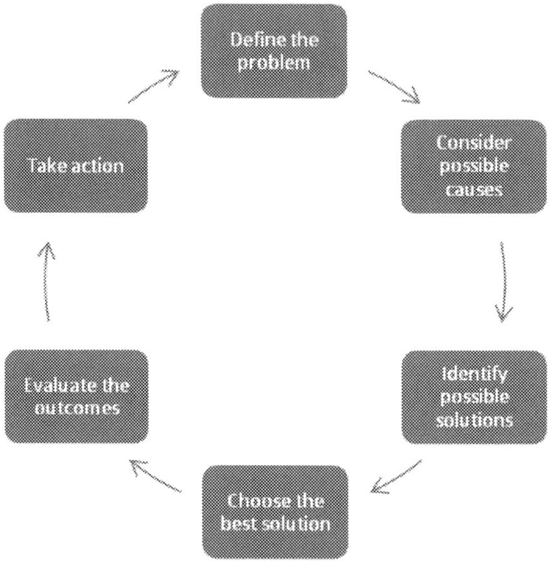

1. **Define the problem:** You need to think about this in specific terms, what is the root problem?

   (a) Are you losing money?
   (b) Are you not making enough money?
   (c) Are you not progressing up levels?
   (d) Are you not enjoying your poker?
   (e) Poker is affecting other aspects of your life?

2. **Consider possible causes:** The more you do this the better you will become at identifying the types of issues that are interfering with your ability to play at your best. What is stopping you from achieving a better result?

   (a) Are you playing distracted?
   (b) Are you playing tired?
   (c) Are you playing outside your bankroll requirements?
   (d) Are you playing at an incorrect level?
   (e) Have you let poker take over your life?

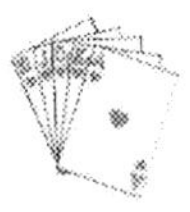

3. **Identify possible solutions:** Look at the individual causes and take time to think closely about what you need to do to remedy the situation.

    (a) Play at particular times of the day or night when the distractions are at a minimum.
    (b) Play only when you are mentally, emotionally and physically prepared to do so.
    (c) Refer to your bankroll management strategy.
    (d) Reduce the amount of poker you are playing.
    (e) Increase the amount of poker you are playing.
    (f) Take a break.
    (g) Talk to fellow players – chat sites or forums.
    (h) Spend some more time studying.

4. **Choose the 'best' solution:** Analyse the information you have gathered and select what you consider to be the best solution as it applies to the problem as you understand it.

5. **Evaluate Outcomes:** Feedback is essential. You need to know that the action you have taken is producing desired results. This is where the spread sheets and your game challenges can provide you with a great deal of information in respect to how your game is going and whether or not you are improving.

6. **Take action:** Take action, move forward, and implement a solution. Do something!!! Now that you have spent time working out what the problem is and what you need to do about it, don't drop the ball and decided it simply requires too much effort. Get in there and get it sorted!

As you can see from the typical problem solving cycle, improvement is continuous. The cycle of learning does not stop and there will always be room to better yourself. The moment you find yourself believing you have one aspect of the game under control; it is generally the time when you need to be working harder, on another aspect. At least this has been my experience.

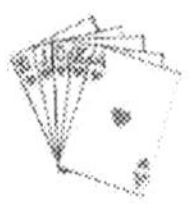

In addition to working through your problem cycle you must continue to:-

1. Be willing to do what others won't.

2. Not worry about what your peers are doing or at what level they are playing. "Keeping up with the Jones" will send you broke. Don't confuse this with looking to other players whose standards you can learn from, this is important.

3. Read another book, magazine article or watch a DVD, when the last one did not help.

4. Move through levels accordingly and stick to your plan, especially when the temptation not to do so hounds you.

5. Remain resolute when considering the second and third principles of the PEA.

6. Play another game, then another, then another ....

7. Keep the game fun. (Lesson 1)

It is very easy to play poker when you are winning and everything you do seems to be going your way but the true test of character comes when you are losing or your game is progressing badly.

This is when you need to step up, not throw in the towel, look at your game and spend some time working out what the issues are.

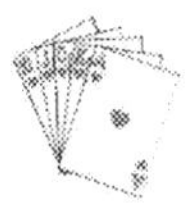

Element 2: Education

"Ignorance is the parent of fear . . ."

Herman Melville
(American novelist and poet.)

Education is defined as "The act or process of imparting or acquiring general knowledge, developing the powers of reasoning and judgment, and generally of preparing oneself or others intellectually for mature life". The importance of education cannot be overestimated! Knowledge is the most valuable commodity a person can possess or invest in. Education empowers us as individuals to think, question and see beyond the obvious. Education expands your horizons and provides you with a better understanding of the world around you and how things work. It increases your confidence giving you more direction and ability to solve problems or deal with issues. I believe education is fundamental to success.

It is important that we as poker players are competent in the basic skills associated with the game. To ensure this level of competence is maintained, we need to assess our personal knowledge, skills and behaviours against those of other players. (For want of a better way of saying it – "Industry Standard".) It is only through comparison that we can determine whether we are competent in the activities and tasks we carry out. Then we can determine what type or processes of education we need to adopt in order to improve those areas.

Poker is brutal in the sense that we generally measure our success in very simple terms - Am I winning money or am I losing money? I can say though that I have walked away from games having lost money but knowing I have been successful. Why? As part of your poker education you are going to play games on occasion that are above your level, or in formats that you are not familiar with. You are going to experiment with strategies, and you will challenge yourself or push your boundaries. In each of these instances the game is not so much about winning (which is nice) but more about learning something else about your game. When you leave a game in the money or not, if you have learned something about poker, your play or that of others, then you have finished successfully.

It is through the use of books, magazines, DVD's, television shows, websites, coaching, mentoring training schools tutorials, chat sites and

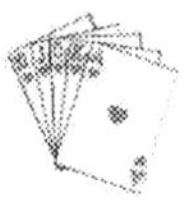

bulletin boards that we will begin or continue the process of education. Once we go down this path we will be able to expand on areas that we have identified as important to our game or simply interest us.

We can look to:-

1. **Improve our technical knowledge** - Gain a better understanding of the rules, strategies and types of games, resources and technology available.

2. **Increase our knowledge about the industry** – Immerse ourselves in the world of poker, its players, the tournaments and what is happening both politically and socially.

3. **Advance ability to communicate** - Identify and build upon our ability to communicate at both local and broader levels. For example, establishing networks on line or within your community.

4. **Build on our ability to problem solve** – Explore methods to improve our problem solving abilities, analytical skills or reasoning powers.

5. **Improve our capacity to self-manage** - Another area vital to ensuring that we are playing within our means is our capacity to self-manage. This provides us with opportunities to expand our understanding on such subjects as time and risk management.

6. **Improve our mental and emotional state** – Learn how to relax, meditate, unwind or simply clear our mind. It is important that we grasp how to balance our desire to play with an understanding of what is going on mentally and emotionally. A friend recently asked me if I play poker to relax – No way! I find poker extremely enjoyable but definitely not relaxing. I have methods I use to get into the right frame of mind before I start playing and strategies I use to try to stay there.

7. **Improve our level of discipline** - Given that we recognise the huge role that discipline plays in our poker, it is imperative that we develop the skill. Being aware of your actions while playing will of course help you to improve in this area however there are a multitude of resources that can teach you how to become more disciplined.

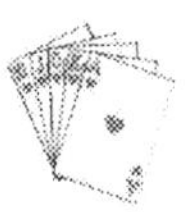

One of the fundamental aspects of education is feedback, (the flow of information to us from others or tools specifically designed to provide us with information about the particulars of our game). Feedback helps us to identify weaknesses as well as strengths, which in turn helps to identify specific aspects of our game that may or may not require attention.

In the realms of poker you will receive feedback in one of two ways:-

1. **Self-Assessment** – This feedback can be drawn from your spreadsheets, game tracking software or simply by monitoring your bankroll. You will analyse the information or results available then follow a typical problem solving cycle as previously discussed. Finally you will re-assess and then repeat the process.

2. **Peer assessment** – Players within your home group, at your local club or bar and other games both on-line and off can occasionally provide you with a benefit in the way of open and honest feedback. I have found it extremely valuable having a "poker partner". In addition to playing poker together we read the same books and magazines, play on the same sites and spend hours discussing various aspects of poker. The beauty of a poker partner is being able to dissect each other's games and provide feedback without fear of upsetting each other. (That's not to say that we have always agreed or haven't had the occasional debate).

It is important that we remain open to feedback. Most of us are happy to receive positive feedback as we like to be told that we are doing / playing well. For the majority of us though, we probably don't respond well to negative feedback, although this can depend on the credibility of the person giving the feedback or how much we respect them. Once we fully comprehend the importance of feedback, accepting it in all its forms becomes easier.

To help, try taking some of the following actions:-

1. **Control your defensiveness** - Two things happen when you become defensive. You close down your ability to take onboard what is being said and often miss the point. You alienate the person or group trying to provide the feedback and you will find that information won't be as forthcoming in the future.

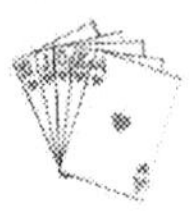

2. **Listen** - Practice all the skills of an effective listener including using body language and facial expressions that encourage the other person to talk. Don't interrupt or demonstrate an impatience that indicates you are simply waiting to have your say.

3. **Suspend judgment** – Don't argue or try influence the person providing the feedback. You require unbiased and open opinions not confrontation. Take with you the message and digest it in your own time and place. This will allow you to remain objective.

4. **Summarise, reflect and respond** - Clarify what is being said, asking questions where required, so that you understand the points being raised. This also lets the person providing the feedback know that you have understood the message. Take time to think about the feedback and respond openly, positively and appropriately.

5. **A second opinion** - Just because a person gives you feedback, doesn't always mean their opinion is right. Check with others to determine the reliability of the feedback. If one person tells you that you play like a fish, you can smile and move on but if ten people say the same thing then maybe you need to swim away and perhaps read a book!

Remember, only you have the ability to decide how you will react to feedback and what you will do with it. Try to show your appreciation to the person providing the feedback by encouraging and supporting comments. The result will be that they feel their opinions are valued and appreciated and they will continue to provide you with an extremely valuable asset in your poker education.

Research Question 12

Which poker pro unknowingly mucked the winning hand in the 2009 World Series of Poker Main Event to a pair of Aces?

What hand did that player muck?

Element 3: Association

"Every man becomes, to a certain degree, what the people he generally converses with are."

Robert Motherwell
(American painter, printmaker and editor)

Association provides a mental connection or relationship between thoughts, feelings and ideas. In the realms of poker association allows us to grow and mature as players. It is through association that we are able to build upon our own ideas, expand on those of others, while developing our own unique style or character. Association breeds success - spending time with a group of millionaires however, is not a guarantee you will become a millionaire. But I can almost guarantee you will walk away better suited to deal with your financial affairs than if you had not had that interaction.

Obviously we are not all in a position where we can spend time with people who are known to be successful in the realms of poker, but the internet is an amazing tool in this regard. The internet opens the door to a range of tools and more importantly, a range of people.

So how do we associate without associating? An interview with a poker legend is as simple as buying their book. We immerse ourselves in all the tools mentioned as part of our education process. We play, read, watch, listen and learn using all of these instruments and at the same time continue to search for resources that are better suited to us, our game and our goals.

MENTORS AND COACHES

One of the best forms of association is to find a mentor or coach. It is not always possible to find someone locally who fits the criteria but there are a multitude of websites that can provide you access to professional poker coaches or mentors. I would highly recommend that you spend some time researching the opportunities that are available.

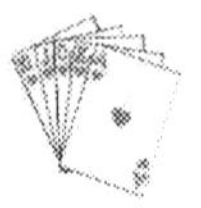

Both coaches and mentors use the same skills and approach, but coaching tends to be more short-term orientated around tasks whereas mentoring is a more long-term relationship.

The personal characteristics I look for in an effective coach or mentor are the abilities to empathise, remain enthusiastic, to listen, remain patient and tactful, be honest as well as processing good feedback skills. I also want my coach / mentor to be positive, enthusiastic, supportive, trusting, focused, goal-orientated, knowledgeable, observant, clear and assertive. What a huge ask! But in reality, when you start looking you will find that there are plenty of people who meet these requirements. As with most things, with a little trial and error you will find what you are looking for.

On finding a good coach or mentor you will gain access to a range of benefits that cannot be understated and some of these benefits include:-

- Acquiring new skills and knowledge;
- Showing more creativity in your game;
- Spending less time playing inappropriate levels or game types;
- Making mistakes in a safe learning environment;
- Having opportunities for challenging and risk-taking activities;
- Developing increased self-confidence;
- Becoming more strategic and goal-oriented;
- Developing an ability to conduct self-assessment of strengths and weaknesses;
- Learning to be patient and disciplined;
- Discovering new support networks with other players;
- Accelerated learning.

This is not a definitive list but we can see that the advantages of having someone on our team with the right experience and knowledge is going to be of enormous benefit. You also have to remember that the relationship is a two-way street and as such you are going to be required to contribute or play your part.

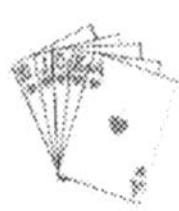

Here are some of the behaviours you will be expected to contribute as part of this relationship.

- Be open and honest;
- Demonstrate that you are consistent, dependable and trustworthy;
- Maintain a cheerful and positive attitude;
- Be willing to ask for help;
- Be open to new ideas and have a willingness to learn;
- Be accepting of feedback;
- Be willing to allot time and resources;
- Be punctual and meet deadlines;
- Be attentive;
- Carry out tasks that have been assigned.

NETWORKING

Networking is another very important step in expanding our knowledge base. It allows us to come together with other like-minded players and use each other to gather resources and information, as well as sharing our experiences. As part of a network you will gain:-

- Access to valuable information;
- Access to diverse skills, knowledge and advice when and where you need it;
- The ability to develop your game;
- Access to contacts;
- Access to discussion groups or regular meetings.

Networks can be established in a wide variety of places and when looking to build your networks try to consider the following:-

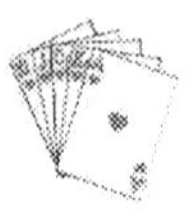

- Family, friends and acquaintances - a great place to start when establishing your home group;
- School or work;
- Night clubs, pubs or bar;
- Sporting clubs;
- Professional associations like “The World Poker Association”.

In this day and age with the explosion of the internet - Facebook, MySpace, Twitter to name but a few - the establishment of a network could not be simpler. If you want to set up networks that go beyond your community then the internet is the perfect tool.

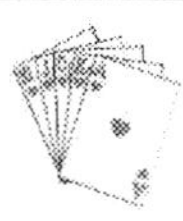

LESSON 10 - A LITTLE MORE REVIEW

"By seeking and blundering we learn."

Wolfgang Goethe
(German writer artist and politician)

Learning Outcomes

In the previous lessons we have come to understand several important factors associated with playing poker such as chip stack, starting hands and table position. In addition we have explored game management, establishing a home game and played a few practice games. Now once again, let us have a bit of fun and see how much you have retained.

Element 1: Multiple Choice Quiz

Element 2: Short Answer Questions

Element 3: True or False Questions

All answers can be found the Fish 'n' Chips Answer Guide on page 229.

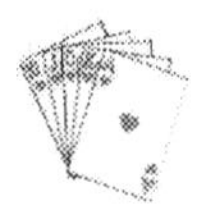

Element 1: Multiple Choice Quiz

Try to answer all of the following fifteen questions by placing the letter of your choice in the box provided. All answers can be found in the answers section at the back of the book

1. The odds or receiving a pair of aces are?

   (A) 235 - 1
   (B) 16 - 2
   (C) 220 - 1
   (D) Impossible

2. A, K is known by what slang name?

   (A) Annie Duke
   (B) Anna Kournikova
   (C) Andrew Korn
   (D) Anton King

3. There are how many possible starting hands?

   (A) 139
   (B) 149
   (C) 159
   (D) 169

4. 7-2 off suit is the worst starting hand in Texas Hold'em, and is it known as?

   (A) The Screwdriver
   (B) The Saw
   (C) The Pliers
   (D) The Hammer

5. The cut off is in what position at the table in relation to the dealer?

   (A) One place right
   (B) Two places right
   (C) One place left
   (D) Two places left

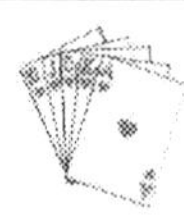

6. A term used to describe how much money I have to play poker with in any given year?

    (A) Bank account
    (B) Bank cheque
    (C) Bankroll
    (D) Bank details

7. Assuming we have $1000 in our bankroll what is the maximum cash game we can play if adhering to our bankroll rules.

    (A) 5c / 10c
    (B) 10c / 20c
    (C) 25c / 50c
    (D) $1 / $2

8. Assuming we have $2000 in our bankroll what is the maximum tournament game we can play in if adhering to our bankroll rules.

    (A) $10
    (B) $25
    (C) $50
    (D) $100

9. The table position that is considered by some to be the hardest to play is what?

    (A) Dealer
    (B) Small Blind
    (C) Cut Off
    (D) Under the Gun

10. What type of rules can we establish to help run our home game

    (A) Home
    (B) Garden variety
    (C) House
    (D) Casino

11. In a typical problem solving cycle, we can do what with a problem?

    (A) Evaluate outcomes
    (B) Take action
    (C) Define
    (D) All of the above

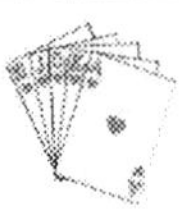

12. A player who plays many hands, often inferior, is usually called what?

    (A) Shifty
    (B) Dave
    (C) Loose
    (D) Wild

13. We accept that poker has many highs and lows. This is referred to as what?

    (A) Pot limit
    (B) Life
    (C) Aggressive
    (D) Variance

14. The truth about where you stand in relation to your wins and losses will only be as good as what?

    (A) Your bankroll
    (B) Your stack size
    (C) The car you drive
    (D) The records you keep

15. Failing to adhere to your bankroll requirements will ultimately cost you what?

    (A) Time
    (B) Patience
    (C) Money
    (D) Enthusiasm

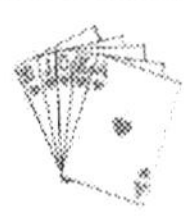

Element 2: Short Answer Questions

Answer the following questions in the areas provided. All answers can be found in the answers section at the back of the book. If you are unsure please review the previous lessons.

1. What are the three main considerations that contribute to how you would play a hand?

2. What are the three most important things required to run a home game?

3. The "PEA" acronym stands for what?

4. Why is 10,2 off suit called "Doyle Brunson"?

5. What is a key process required to maintain your strategy while ensuring you don't exceed your financial limitations?

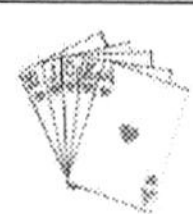

6. When using feedback for your own use, (i.e. taking notes on the game you are playing) your comments should be;

7. What do we do if we use all of our bankroll?

8. In the realms of poker you will receive feedback in one of two ways. What are they?

9. One of the best forms of association is to find a what?

10. Finish the following statement, “We are made to persist ....”

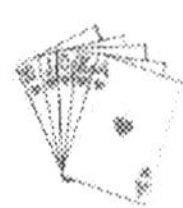

Element 3: True or False

Answer the following true or false questions in the area provided. All answers can be found in the answers section at the back of the book. The answers are drawn from statements or comments in the book.

1. Tracking game results appropriately is an important part of our game?

2. When you first begin to play, it is a good idea to "multi-table"

3. Feedback is important when learning to play poker?

4. The big blind is three times the size of the small blind.

5. It is not necessary to balance tables during poker events.

6. "Association" with other players can be achieved through books

7. Mentors tend to be long-term relationships whereas coaches tend to be task orientated

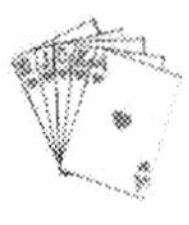

8. Your mental and emotional state is an important consideration prior to the commencement of playing poker.

9. Networking gives is diverse skills and allows us to develop our contacts and game.

10. "Rabbit hunting" is a form of betting.

11. If one person gives you feedback it doesn't mean their feedback is right.

12. Developing an ability to conduct self-assessment of strengths and weaknesses does not relate to poker.

Research Question 13

When was the first World Series of Poker Main Event held, and who was the winner of that event?

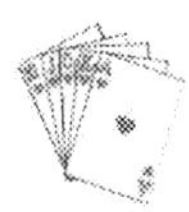

LESSON 11 - LEARNING OUR LANGUAGE

"Language is the light of the mind"

John Mill
(English political philosopher and economist)

Learning Outcomes

In Lesson 11 we are going to spend some time learning the most common phrases and terms associated with Texas Hold'em. I thought it necessary to include a lesson specifically aimed at learning the basic "language" of poker however, it is my hope that by this stage of the book you will already be very familiar with many of the terms we are going to looking at.

In order to achieve your poker goals and become "relatable", it is very important that we understand the words being spoken. Spend some time practising the terminology so you are capable of least holding a basic conversation or understanding the commentary on the late night games.

The words included have been drawn from a variety of sources and by no means represent a definitive collection. Some of these terms are commonly used and some you may only hear occasionally. The words or phrases in italics are the more commonly used ones so that you can prioritise which words or phrases to learn first.

Take your time, learn a bit of the lingo and test yourself using the crosswords I have provided.

Element 1: Studying the Language A - J

Element 2: Crossword Challenge A - J

Element 3: Studying the Language K - Z

Element 4: Crossword Challenge K - Z

All answers can be found the Fish 'n' Chips Answer Guide on page 230.

Element 1: Studying the Language A - J

A

Act - To make a decision. Bet, raise, fold, call or check. "It's Jims turn to act"

Action - This describes when it is a player's turn to play or act. "Action is on Vicky".

Active player - A player still involved in the pot.

Add-On - In some tournaments add-ons are used to re-buy into that tournament so that you may continue to play.

Adjust - This is to change the way you play based on the current circumstances.

Advertising - A player makes an obvious play in order to sway the outcome of a hand.

Aggressive - An aggressive player is one who is involved in a lot of hands and usually bets or raises. "Ken is playing aggressive tonight"

Air - This refers to a card that is of no help to any player. "The 3 of clubs on the river is complete *air* to all players".

All-In - This is when a player commits all of his chips to the pot. "I am *all in*!"

American Airlines - A pair of aces, also known as pocket rockets.

Ammunition - A slang term for chips

Ante - An ante is a bet or commitment to the pot that must be made by all players in order to play in a poker hand.

Arsenal - A series of moves or strategies usually employed by a player.

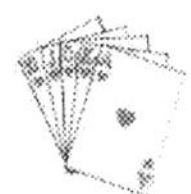

B

Backdoor - Either catching both the turn and river card to make a drawing hand or to make a hand that was not intended

Bad beat - When a hand that is considered the underdog beats a hand that is heavily favoured to win.

Bank - The person responsible for distributing chips, keeping track of the buy-ins, and paying winners at the end of the game.

Bankroll - The amount of money that a player has to wager over the duration of given period of time (usually a year).

Behind - Not currently having the best hand. "The flop has come down and Jack is behind."

Bet - Any money wagered during the play of a hand.

Betting structure - A specific set of rules which govern how much is required to be bet in a given game at a given point.

Big blind (BB) - The larger of the two blinds.

Big blind special (BBS) - A player in the big blind is dealt weak hole cards, then ends up making the best hand because he or she was able to see the flop for free.

Blank - A community card, of no apparent value

Bleed - To continually lose small amounts, to the point that it becomes a large loss.

Blind - A type of forced bet, put into the pot before any of the cards are dealt.

Bluff - To bet on an inferior hand hoping your opponent will fold.

Board - The set of face up community cards

Bobtail - An open-ended or "outside" straight draw.

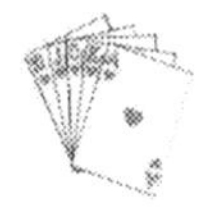

Bone - A chip, usually of small denomination.

Bot - Short for "robot". A computer program that plays poker.

Box - The chip tray in front of a house dealer, therefore house dealer's position.

Boxed card - A card that is face-up in a deck during the deal .

Break - To end a session of play.

Bubble - The point at which only one player must be eliminated before all others win some money.

Buck - A token used to mark the position of the dealer.

Bullet - An ace or another term for a chip.

Bully - to continuously bluff or a player who does so.

Bum deal - A misdeal.

Bump - To raise.

Burn - To discard the top card from the deck, face down.

Busted - Did not complete a hand such as chasing a fifth card to make a flush and not "hitting" it. Also means to be out of chips.

Button - A token, usually white, used to mark the position of the dealer.

Buy - The act of bluffing. "He bought (buy) the pot".

Buy-in - The amount required to pay to enter a tournament or game.

C

Call - To match the latest bet or raised amount.

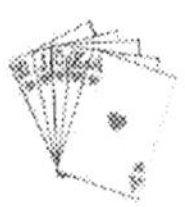

Calling station - A weak player who frequently checks and calls, but rarely raises.

Case cards - The last available card of a certain type.

Catch - To receive the required cards on a draw.

Catch up - To successfully complete a draw.

Centre pot - The first pot created during a poker hand. (Note - see also "Side pot".)

Chase - To continue to play a drawing hand. For example, a player needs another card to make a straight and continues to chase that card.

Check - To pass or not bet.

Check out - To fold without a requirement to do so.

Check-raise - To check, and then re-raise when a player preceding you bets.

Chip - Token representing money used for betting.

Chip along - To continue to bet or call the minimum required in order to remain in play.

Chip dumping - A type of collusion that happens during tournaments, two or more players go all-in early giving the winner a large amount of chips.

Chip up - To exchange lower-denomination chips for higher-denomination chips.

Chop - To split a pot or winnings because of a tie, split-pot game, or player agreement.

Coffeehouse - To comment in an annoying or deceptive manner during a game.

Cold - Unlucky – not hitting your desired cards.

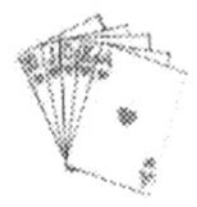

Cold call - To call more than one bet in a single play. For example; a player raises one big blind, any other player must call two bets to continue playing.

Cold deck - A deck that has been arranged then brought into a game to produce a specific outcome.

Collusion - A form of cheating where two or more players act or work together.

Colour up - To exchange small-denomination chips for larger ones.

Community card - A card dealt face-up to the centre of the table that can be used by all players in the action.

Completion - To raise a small bet up to the amount of what would be a normal-sized bet.

Connector - A starting hand where the two cards are one apart in rank. For example: 7-8 or Q-K

Crack - To beat a better hand (Crack Aces).

Cut - Take some of the cards off the top of a deck and move them to the bottom.

Cut Off - The seat immediately to the right of the dealer button.

D

Dead hand - A player's hand that cannot be played. (A hand is declared dead if that player announces that they are folding when faced with a bet or a raise.)

Deal - To distribute cards to players.

Dealer - The person who is dealing the cards.

Deep - A large amount of money in play or having been lost.

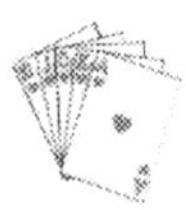

Deuce - A card with the rank of 2.

Discard - To take a previously dealt card out of play.

Dog - A player with a smaller chance of winning compared to other players. (More commonly known as “Underdog”.)

Dominated Hand - A hand being played that will almost always lose to a better hand.

Donation - A call made by a player who expects to lose.

Donkey - Derogatory term for an inexperienced, or unskilled, player. “Fred, you really are a useless donkey.” (See also “Fish”.)

Down card - A card that is dealt facedown.

Draw - To stay in a hand in hopes of improving, usually to a straight or flush.

Drawing dead - To play a drawing hand that will lose even if you make your hand.

Drawing live - Drawing to a hand that will win if successful.

Drawing thin - Chasing a draw when facing poor odds.

Dumb end - The bottom end of a straight. For example:- you hold 6–2 and 7–8-9 flops. The turn is a 10. You know have the dumb end as opposed to the high end straight. (See also “Idiot end”.)

Dump, dumped - To lose a large amount of your stack to another player in short succession.

E

Early position - The player/s who bet first are said to be in early position.

Exposed card - A card whose face has been deliberately or accidentally revealed.

F

Family pot - A deal where most, if not all players called the first opening bet.

Fast play - To play a hand aggressively.

Fifth Street - The last community card dealt to the board. Commonly referred to as "The River".

Fill, Fill up - To successfully get the card you require for your draw.

Fire - To make the opening bet of a round.

Fish - Derogatory term for an inexperienced, or unskilled, player (See also Donkey).

Flash - To show the bottom card of the deck while shuffling.

Flat call - To call in a situation where that player might be expected to raise.

Flop, (The) - The first three community cards dealt.

Forward motion – When a player picks up some chips and takes their hand forward towards the pot as if to make a bet.

Fox hunt - To reveal the next card that would have come up, after a hand has completed.

Free card - A community card dealt to the board that did not require a player to call a bet.

Free roll - A tournament with no entry fee.

Freeze out - A winner-take-all tournament.

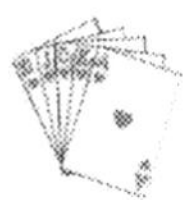

G

Grind, Grinder - A player who earns a living by making small profits over a long period of time through consistent and conservative play.

Gutshot - An inside straight draw. For example:- you have 9-10 and the flop comes down Q-8-2. You require a Jack to make the straight.

Gypsy - To enter the pot cheaply by just calling the blind rather than raising. (Commonly referred to as "Limping".)

H

Hammer – To hammer means to bet and raise aggressively. "The Hammer" refers to a starting hand consisting of a 7-2 off suit.

Hand - A single round or game.

Hand for hand - So that an equal number of hands are played on all tables, (tournament play), play is halted as each table finishes a hand until all tables have completed.

Hard - Aggressive and uncompromising play.

Heads Up - Only two players in a hand or remaining at the table.

High end - The top end of a straight. For example:- you hold K–3 and Q–9-10 flops. The turn is a J. You know have the high end straight.

Hit - To receive the community cards you had hoped for. "I hit the flop."

Hole, Hole cards - The two cards you have been dealt. Your hole cards.

Home game - A game played at a private venue.

House - The establishment running the game.

Horse - A player financially backed by someone else.

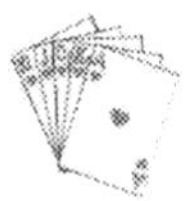

I

Ice - A cold deck.

Idiot end - The bottom end of a straight (more commonly known as the "Dumb end".)

Improve - To get a better hand as the community cards fall.

Inside, Inside straight - See "Gutshot"

In the money - To place high enough in a tournament to get prize money.

Irregularity - An abnormal condition of play.

Isolation - To play aggressively in order to drive out all but one specific opponent.

J

Jack it up - To raise.

Jackpot - A large pool of money collected then awarded by the house for a specific event or result.

Research Question 14

What are the odds that any random
Texas Hold'em flop will contain
a three of a kind?

Element 2: Crossword Challenge A – J

Let's see how much you have learned. Complete the following crossword and test your own knowledge. Good Luck!!

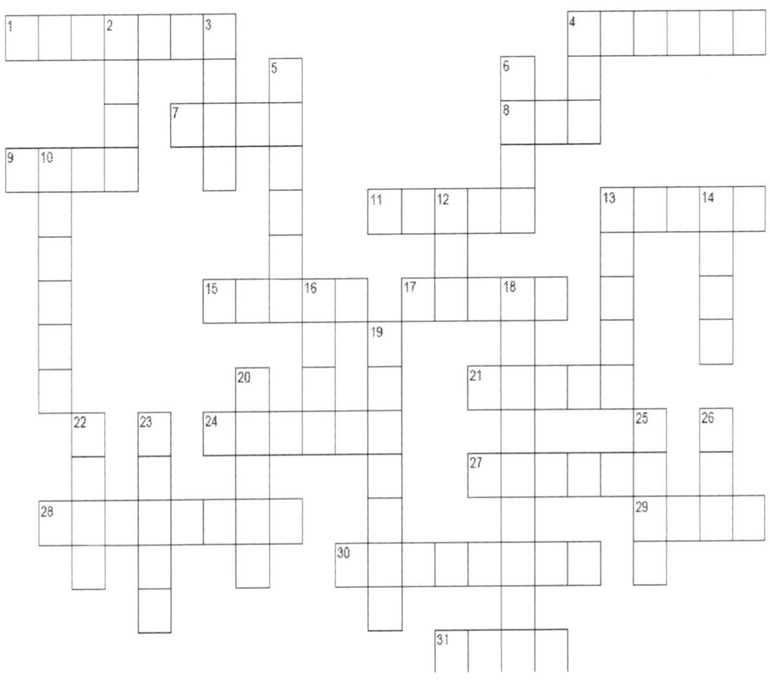

ACROSS

1 To take a previously dealt card out of play.

4 A token, usually white, used to mark the position of the dealer.

7 A single round or game.

8 To make a decision. Bet, raise, fold, call or check.

9 To split a pot or winnings because of a tie, split-pot game, or player agreement.

11 A community card, of no apparent value

13 To bet on an inferior hand hoping your opponent will fold.

15 To receive the required cards on a draw.

17 To beat a better hand.

21 A type of forced bet, put into the pot before any of the cards are dealt.

24 An ace or another term for a chip

27 The point at which only one player must be eliminated before all others win some money.

28 A tournament with no entry fee.

29 A bet or commitment to the pot that must be made in order to play in a poker hand.

30 A call made by a player who expects to lose.

31 A chip, usually of small denomination.

DOWN

2 A token representing money used for betting.
3 To stay in a hand in hopes of improving, usually to a straight or flush.
4 Any money wagered during the play of a hand.
5 This is to change the way you play based on the current circumstances.
6 The person responsible for distributing chips, keeping track of the buy-ins, and paying winners at the end of the game.
10 To bet and raise aggressively. A starting hand consisting of a 7-2 offsuit.
12 This refers to a card that is of no help to any player.
13 The set of face up community cards
14 Derogatory term for an inexperienced, or unskilled, player, as in DonkeyFlash To show the bottom card of the deck while shuffling.
16 To match the latest bet or raised amount.
18 A form of cheating where two or more players act or work together.
19 An inside straight draw. For example, you have 9h & 10h and the flop comes down Qc, 8s & 2d. You require a Jack to make the straight.
20 To continuously bluff , or a player who does so.
22 To discard the top card from the deck, face down.
23 To pass or not bet.
25 To distribute cards to players .
26 To receive the community cards you had hoped for. "I hit the flop"

Element 3: Studying the Language K – Z

K

Keep honest - To call a final bet while not expecting to win, with the aim of discouraging future bluffs. "I am going to call you John, just to keep you honest"

Kicker - A card used for deciding ties. (See Lesson 2 – Types of Hands.)

Kitty - Money collected from games or pots to be used for another purpose.

L

Laydown - To fold a good hand in the face of a better hand or opponent.

Leak - A weakness in your game

Limit - The minimum or maximum amount of a bet.

Limp - To enter a pot by simply calling instead of raising.

Live - Remains able to be raised.

Loose - A player who plays many hands, often inferior.

Loose cannon - A player who is not afraid to bet, or "gamble".

M

Maniac - A loose and aggressive player.

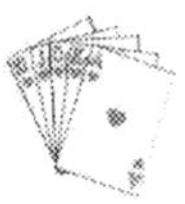

Misdeal - A deal which is ruined for some reason and must be re-dealt.

Muck - The pile of discarded cards after players have folded their hands or the act of not revealing one's cards after a player has won.

N

No-limit - A betting structure where players may wager as much as they like.

Nuts (The) - To hold the best hand.

O

Off suit - Cards that are not of the same suit.

One-Gap - A starting hand with two cards two apart in rank. For example: 10, Q or 6, 8.

Open - To bet first.

Outs - Cards remaining in the deck that can improve a players hand.

Outside straight - A draw to a straight with a single missing rank at either end, for example, 10-J-Q-K requires an ace or a 9. Also known as an "open-end straight", or "two-way straight draw".

Outrun - To beat another player.

Overcall - To call a bet after one or more others players have already called.

Over-card - A community card with a higher rank than a player's pocket pair.

Over-pair - A pocket pair higher than any card on the flop. For example, you have J-J and the flop comes 9-8-3, then you have an over-pair.

P

Paint - The picture or face cards in a deck - Jacks, Queens and Kings.

Passive - An opponent who rarely raises.

Pat - A hand that is complete. Full house, straight etc.

Play the Board - To play a hand to the river then show your cards only to find the community cards hold the best hand for all players. The pot would then be split.

Pocket - The two cards dealt to you in Texas Hold'em. [See Hole Cards.]

Poker face - A player's face that does not reveal anything about the cards being held.

Position bet - A bet that is made due to the strength of that player's position rather than the strength of the cards held.

Post - To make the required small or big blind bet.

Pot - The money or chips that players in the hand can win from the bets to that point.

Pot committed - A situation where you are forced to call the rest of your stack because of the size of the pot and your remaining chips.

Pot limit - A betting limit where the maximum amount a player can bet is the amount in the pot.

Pot odds - The size of the pot compared to the bet. For example a pot contain $100 and you need to bet $10 to stay in the game you are getting pot odds of 10:1 to play.

Protect - To put more money into a pot so that the money that you've already put in isn't lost.

Push - To put yourself all-in.

Put On - To pick a hand you believe a player has for the purposes of continuing to play your hand.

Q

Quads - Four of a kind.

R

Rack - A collection of 100 chips of the same denomination.

Rags - Worthless cards.

Ragged - A flop that doesn't appear to help anybody very much.

Rail - The sideline at a poker table.

Rainbow - Three or four cards of different suits.

Raise - To put in more money than the existing bet.

Rake - A fee taken by the house.

Rank - The numerical value of a card.

Re-buy - An option to buy back into a tournament after you've lost all your chips.

Re-deal - To deal a hand again.

Re-raise - To raise after a player has been raised.

Represent - To play as if you hold a certain hand.

Ring game - A non-tournament poker game played for stakes.

River - The fifth (community) card dealt face up on the board.

Rock - A passive and tight player.

Rockets - A pair of aces.

Runner - A tournament entrant, a contestant.

Runner-runner - A hand made by hitting two consecutive cards on the Turn and River.

Rush - A player who has won several big pots is said to be on a rush.

S

Sandbag - To play your hand slowly to gain an advantage in a tournament with a timed blinds structure.

Satellite - A tournament where the prize is a free entrance to another (larger) tournament.

Scare Card - A community card that may change the best hand into a non winning hand.

Second Pair - A pair with the second highest card on the flop.

Semi-bluff - A large bet on a drawing hand.

Short Stack - A number of chips that is relatively low compared to the other players at the table.

Set - Three of a kind with two of the cards in the player's hole cards and the third card in the community cards.

Showdown - When the cards are revealed at the end of the game.

Side pot - A separate pot created if one player has gone all-in and the other players continue to bet.

Slow play - A strategy whereby good cards are played conservatively, with hopes that other players will keep playing the hand and build a larger pot.

Small Blind (SB) - The smaller of two blind bets. The small blind is generally half the big blind.

Small blind special - A situation where a player is dealt weak hole cards in the small blind, but ends up making the best hand because it was not expensive to continue to play.

Smooth Call - To call usually with a strong hand.

Soft-Play - To go easy on another player at the table.

Splash the pot - To throw your chips into the pot in a disorderly fashion.

Split pot - Usually the result of a tie, each player tied takes an equal share.

Stack - A collection of 20 chips of the same denomination, usually arranged in an orderly column.

Stakes - The amount a player buys in for and can bet.

Steal - Usually means to bluff. "Once again Ken is out to steal the blinds"

Steam - Playing recklessly when one is frustrated.

Stop 'n' Go - A play where you call a raise, then bet on the next card.

String bet - A bet such that a player uses two separate motions to make a bet without verbally declaring your intention.

Structured - Describes specific betting structure in poker games.

Suck out - To draw a winning hand despite poor odds.

Suited - Cards that are of the same suit.

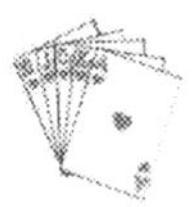

T

Tell - An action or comment that gives away information about one's cards.

Tight - A player who rarely calls.

Tilt - To make reckless betting decisions as a result of frustration.

Time - A request by a player to suspend play while he decides what he's going to do.

Toke - A small amount of money given to the dealer by the winner of a pot.

Trips - Three of a kind with one of the cards in the player's hole cards and the other two in the community cards.

Turn - The fourth community card in Texas Hold'em.

U

Under the Gun - The playing position to the direct left of the blinds.

Underdog - A person or hand not mathematically favoured to win a pot.

Up card - A card that is dealt face up.

Up the ante - Increase the stake.

V

Value bet - A bet made for the purpose of increasing the size of the pot. The player wants this bet to be called.

Variance - A measure of the up and down swings your bankroll goes through.

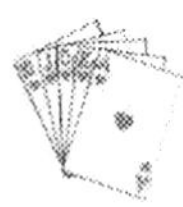

Element 4: Crossword Challenge K - Z

Let's see how much you have learned. Complete the following crossword and test your own knowledge. Once complete use this lesson to check your answers. Good Luck!!

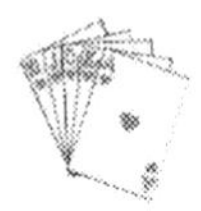

ACROSS

1 Usually means to bluff.
3 Worthless cards.
6 Cards that are not of the same suit.
7 The fourth community card in Texas hold 'em.
9 A card used for deciding ties. (Note chapter - hand examples.)
12 To make the required small or big blind bet.
13 To deal a hand again.
15 (The) To Hold the best hand
16 A player who rarely calls.
18 Four of a kind.
21 To fold a good hand in the face of a better hand or opponent.
22 An action or comment that gives away information about one's cards.
24 Three of a kind. Two cards on the board.
25 The two cards dealt to you in Texas Hold 'em.
26 To bet first.

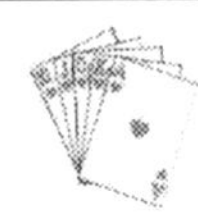

DOWN

1 A collection of 20 chips of the same denomination, usually arranged in an orderly column.

2 To put yourself all-in.

3 To put in more money than the existing bet.

4 Three of a kind with two of the cards in the player's hole cards and the third card in the community cards.

5 A card that is dealt face up.

6 A community card with a higher rank than a player's pocket pair.

8 A pair of aces

10 A player who plays many hands, often inferior.

11 The face cards in a deck - Jacks, Queens, and Kings,

14 A deal which is ruined for some reason and must be redealt.

17 The fifth (community) card dealt face up on the board.

19 An opponent who rarely raises.

20 The money or chips that players in the hand can win from the bets to that point.

23 A weakness in your game

24 To make reckless betting decisions as a result of frustration.

LESSON 12 - WHERE TO GO FROM HERE?

"The route to a destination is dictated by the start location of the one that makes the journey."

Hanno Langenhoven
(Head of Spiritual Development and Retreat Centre)

Learning Outcomes

Congratulations!!! You have progressed through this book and are now well and truly armed with the information you require to begin taking your game to the next level and beyond. It is now time to indulge your hobby, passion or potential career and begin what is really Stage Two of your learning process.

In this final chapter I want to consolidate what it is you have learned and "bring it all home".

Element 1: Following the "PEA"

Element 2: Play, Play, Play

Element 3: My Top Ten Tips

Element 1: Following the "PEA"

Following on from the "PEA" principle, we will now take a look at what to do and where to go from here.

1. JOIN AN ON-LINE POKER SITE

Start playing for play money or get into some low stake real money cash or tournament games. Try some of the challenges I have outlined in Lesson 8. When considering a poker site you need to think about the type of functionality and ease of use you require in your poker game. In doing so I suggest you consider the following:-

(a) **Software used** - Do you want to use a downloadable version of the software or one which runs in your browser? Clearly you are going to want reliability, a program that won't give you constant drop-outs or leave you dealing with glitches. While playing on-line do you want access to statistics such as number of players, average chip count, your current position or upper and lower chip stack sizes? Is it important that you have the ability to chat or disable chat? Do you want the option of playing multiple tables?

(b) **Games available** – Most sites run various types of poker games but a few are limited in their variety because of the number of players who use the site. What sort of variation do you require in your game options? Do you require access to play money, multiple types of tournaments and/or cash games? Look for sites that offer a good selection of levels.

(c) **Bonuses** – Are joining or playing bonuses important to you and if so, what type of bonuses do you expect or like? Are very important player (VIP) rewards essential or not?

(d) **Customer support** – Does the site have good customer support? Do you have 24/7 access to this support and is it provided over the phone, via email and/or SMS? Do you receive a response in a helpful and timely manner?

(e) **Banking options** – What type of banking facilities are available - such as credit card, bank card or Pay Pal deposits? Does the company have a streamlined, efficient and timely payout system?

(f) **Player usage and competition** - This is a balancing act. You want to find a site that has quite a few players but by the same token you want to play with players from a variety of levels. I want to make money but I also I want to be challenged by players at a higher levels.

Research here is the key and there are several websites that you can visit which review poker sites. These websites can provide unbiased opinions as to which sites meet the majority of a player's needs.

Personally I use two sites. Actually I did have three but the US Government (on a day that is now known as "Black Friday") eliminated Full Tilt as my third option, at least for the moment. (A good research topic though.) After surfing the internet to find recommendations from various sites, as well as having tried several sites personally, these are my top five picks:-

(1) www.pokerstars.com

(2) www.pokerstars.net

(3) www.888pokeraustralia.com.

(4) www.titanpoker.com

(5) www.carbonpoker.ag

2. JOIN A LOCAL GAME

Join either a private one or a game in your local club or pub.

3. ESTABLISH A HOME GAME

If you have not done so, join or create your own home group using the guide in Lesson 8 - Element 3.

4. WATCH SOME MOVIES.

There is a difference of opinion over which movies are considered to be the top poker movies of all time. I have watched quite a few, both good and bad. I am sure you will be looking for others once you have worked your way through my recommendations, but in my opinion, the following movies are a great place to start:-

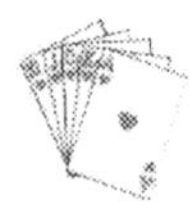

(a) **Rounders** - John Dahl's 1998 film starring Matt Damon, Edward Norton and John Malkovich floats to the top for most poker players as one of the best (if not the best) Texas Hold'em movies made to date.

This is the story of a young gambler and clean-cut law student, Mike McDermott (Matt Damon), who loses his entire life savings to Russian club owner Teddy KGB (John Malkovich) and decides to distance himself from the world of poker and return to his studies while working as a janitor. He is soon convinced to begin playing high stakes poker again in order to help a friend who has just recently been released from prison and acquired a large debt with loan sharks. The story is action packed from game to game until the inevitable show down between Mike and Teddy climaxing in an awesome last hand. Rounders is complete with interesting characters and a plot which will draw you in, especially as a poker player.

(b) **Deal** – This will no doubt be debated one of the best, as the movie did not seem to get a great deal of positive reviews or recognition. A 2008 Gil Cates Jr. movie starring Burt Reynolds, Bret Harrison and Maria Mason. Personally, I loved the story and thought the movie, although a bit predictable was entertaining and exciting.

The story revolves entirely around Texas Hold'em No Limit making it a must see in my opinion. It explores the story of an ex-gambler who, while desperately wishing to relive some of his former glory, decides to mentor a bright college student in the finer details of Texas Hold'em. Soon the teacher finds himself being drawn into the World Series of Poker Championships, and it is here that he must now face his protégé and the inevitable battle for recognition at the highest of poker levels.

(c) **High Roller: The Stu Ungar Story (2005)** - Widely regarded as the world's best ever professional poker and gin rummy player, Stuart Ungar, (aka "The Kid") is only one of two people to have won the World Series of Poker three times and the only person to have won Amarillo Slim's Super Bowl of Poker three times. "Stuey" was born on 8 September 1953 and died as a result of addiction and excess in November 1998. "High Roller" recounts the life of this extraordinary card player who grew up with

affiliations to the mob, a compulsion to consume and a drive to win. The movie portrays yet another example of fame and fortune crashing to an end because of addiction, bad choices and excess.

What makes this movie a necessity to watch is not just that it loosely chronicles the life and times of this legendary poker player but it also raises an interesting point. To be seriously thought of as the greatest player of all time, must we also contemplate our conduct away from the poker table? Should we consider the impact we have on other players, how we contribute to our game and the influence we may have on others -, not to mention bankroll management? A very entertaining movie and one that I feel should be mentioned as a movie to see in order to further expand your understanding of the game and appreciation of the pitfalls.

(d) **All In: The Poker Movie -** This 2012 documentary by Douglas Tirola delves into a brief history of poker and more specifically Texas Hold'em. In doing so we are introduced to a wide variety of professional players, sports writers and actors who all have something to contribute to the topic at hand –

> *Why has Texas Hold'em Poker exploded over the past years and why, for so many, has poker become the way to chase that dream of fame and fortune?*

I actually postponed publication of this book knowing that this DVD was due to be released and I must say that I was not disappointed. In addition to providing the beginner with a brief history of poker and discussions ranging from the "Hole Cam" to "Chris Moneymaker's winning of the 2003 World Series", you are also introduced to a host of names and personalities that as a poker player you really should be familiar with.

5. READ SOME BOOKS.

Actually what I should be saying here is read ***lots*** of books. There are hundreds out there – and another one has just been added to the pile (Mine!) I have read quite a lot of books about Texas Hold'em - some exceptional, some very average and a whole lot in between. There are several books which are recommended almost universally

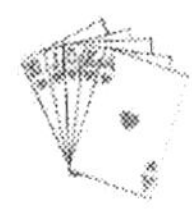

by poker players and I would recommend that you read these as a matter of course.

They are generally regarded as books that every serious player should read and they are as follows:-

- Caro's Book of Poker Tells;
- Sklansky's - The Theory of Poker;
- Harrington on Hold'em – Volumes. 1, 2 and 3;
- Phil Gordon's - The Real Deal;
- Phil Gordon's - Little Green Book;
- Doyle Brunson's Super System.

The very first book I read was Phil Gordon's Little Green Book and I must say that this gave me a great start to my game. This book was passed around our home group and provided a great deal of inspiration and guidance to all the players that read it.

After more than four years of reading (with plenty more years to come I'm sure) I would like mention the books that I feel have had the greatest influence on my game and my general approach to poker to this point:-

(a) **Caro's Book of Poker Tells –** Although a bit dated, this is a book that should be present in any poker player's library as it deals with a vital aspect of poker - the "Tell". As the title suggests, Mike Caro focuses on signals or tells given off by poker players who are unaware they are doing so - from players who are "acting", some general tells and the types of tells players need to look and listen out for. It is a book with plenty of illustrations and clear explanations. The only drawback being is that it does not address the type of tells you will experience on-line. Having said that, the information contained within the pages is invaluable and will go a long way toward improving your game.

Personally, I find tells an extremely interesting aspect of poker and it is an area that I am always keen to learn more about. As such I have read several books on tells and body language. Given that this area of the game is so important I would suggest

that you also dedicate a reasonable amount of time and energy into learning more about this facet of the game.

(b) **Alan N. Schoonmaker's Poker Winners are Different -** What I really enjoyed about this book is that it focuses on the mental issues associated with the game and discusses at length what a player should be doing instead of what they should not. The book explores habits and mindsets that the winning poker player should be adopting in order to continue to play successfully. It includes several exercises and thought provoking questions that help you, as a player, to really understand what it is you want to achieve from the game. It also gives you clear guidance as to what is required to achieve it.

Without doubt, this book has had a positive impact on my playing ability, mental focus and general attitude to players and the game alike. Rarely now do I scream, "you F*^#%@ Fish!! How could you play that cr@p?" I now accept and expect plays and players from all walks of life and all levels of ability. After all, who am I to judge? My learning curve is still climbing steeply and in the realms of poker, I am still a little "fish" in a big pond.

(c) **T.J Cloutier's How To Win The Championship: Hold'em Strategies for The Final Table -** T.J Cloutier is considered to be one of the greatest tournament players in the world. In his book he provides specific advice on how to get to the final table where the big money is made and then what is required to win it. The main reason I love this book is because it is not technical. Cloutier explains every action or point in a way that is easy to understand while making the themes relatable. This book had and continues to have a huge impact on my game.

Given all I have discussed in relation to the importance of body language and understanding your opponents, I would recommend that you invest time and money into developing this skill. By far the biggest collection of books in my Poker arsenal relate to body language. This is because over the past few years I have come to understand that the more I play poker, the more important it becomes to understand body language and tells. In addition to reading several body language books written by the Poker Pros, I have also read several books by Allan Pease, known internationally as "Mr. Body Language". Without a doubt, these books have helped improve my

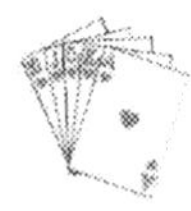

game and I would recommend his "The Definitive Book of Body Language" as a must read.

6. SUBSCRIBE TO A MAGAZINE OR TWO

I have been subscribing to "Bluff" magazine for the past couple of years while my poker partner has been reading "Card Player". We have both benefitted enormously from the articles in these magazines. Not only do you get a keen insight into what is going on in the poker world but the advice and guidance you have access to is invaluable.

7. INVEST IN SOME POKER TRACKING SOFTWARE

This type of software will replace your tracking sheets and the programs available have a far greater functionality and variety in relation to targeting or tracking specific areas of your game. I am not going to go into too much detail about the options available here as this is not an area I have spent a lot of time researching. To do the subject any justice an entire lesson could be dedicated to it.

That being said, I have used "Hold'em Manager" and found it to be extremely useful with an enormous range of options. When time permits, I will look into learning how to use this program properly and explore what other tracking software is currently available. In the meantime, I would suggest that if software is something you are considering then this is a good place to start or perhaps research for yourself what is currently out there.

Research Question 15

What's the nickname of Daniel Negreanu?

Element 2: Play, Play, Play

Play poker!!!

Play a little bit more,

Then, you guessed it ... Play some more!

"Practice makes perfect" and
Element 2 speaks for itself.

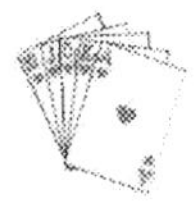

Element 3: My Top Ten Tips

For all the reading, chat sites, blogs, home games, on-line matches and internet surfing I have done over the past four years, several points consistently rise to the surface. These top ten tips are not so much my personal recommendations, rather they represent a collection of opinions that most players would agree are required to improve your game.

I have no doubt whatsoever that if you incorporate some, if not all, of these tips into your poker life then your game is going to continually improve.

1. **Play Within Your Bankroll -** I have harped on enough about bankroll but the reality is that not managing your bankroll is the single easiest way to destroy your ability to play effective poker and / or lose your love for the game (not to mention your money!).

2. **Play at Your Correct Level -** This is as much about ensuring that you are playing within your bankroll requirements as it is about ensuring that you are playing games that are within your skill level. You will progress through levels given time, patience and practice and rushing the process will cost you dearly in the long run.

3. **Don't Play Under the Influence –** The surest way to lose all your money is to play under the influence of alcohol or drugs. I have seen players win occasionally when inebriated but I can guarantee you that playing in any state less than completely clear-headed is going to cost you big in the long run. In addition to placing your finances at risk, playing in this state reeks of "fish" because you are telling everyone at the table from the onset that you are not serious about poker and you are just an easy target.

4. **Don't Play While Out of Balance –** I have to admit that this is one of my biggest challenges and quite often I find myself playing when I really know that shouldn't. Playing in a mental or emotional state that is anything other than prepared will cut into your bank account. So often the scene is not completely set for a good game of poker – "I might have a quick game after work or before dinner" - "I am feeling a little stressed, a game will fix that" - "I have just had an

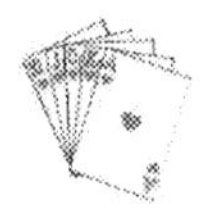

argument" - "I am bored" - "I am tired" – "I am angry". Get yourself mentally and emotionally prepared each and every time before you play. If you can you learn how to do this effectively you are well on your way to making money instead of chucking it away.

5. **Play With Grace** – Poker is a very emotional game and players can be extremely passionate about playing. As a poker player I put a lot of effort into trying to keep my feelings or reactions in check, although I will admit that I am not always successful. I know players who are completely unaware that their behaviour at the table is unacceptable, even after being told. By demonstrating to other players that you are making an effort to play with grace and composure you are leading by example and showing a level of maturity and discipline that is needed to become a good poker player.

6. **Play Honestly and With Integrity** - Wherever money is involved the green eyed monster that is greed will occasionally raise its ugly head. Whenever you play, you should do so honestly and with integrity. If you are running a home game (which I hope by this stage you are), it is vital that you run an above-board game. Stealing or cheating does nothing for your game, nothing for your friendships and is yet another example of a player who is not serious about playing good poker.

7. **Adopt the "PEA"** – Put the principal of the "PEA" into your poker ambitions. Following the guidelines I have detailed in Lesson 9 in relation to success will improve your game and help you to achieve the goals and dreams you desire.

8. **Accept the Facts** – You need to accept some very straightforward facts about poker and if you can keep these points into your mind and game they will go a long way to help become a better player:-

   (a) There are always going to be better players than you, including some of your friends;

   (b) Poker does contain an element of luck and you will experience bad beats;

(c) Poker players come from all walks of life with varying levels of skills, attitudes and temperaments;

(d) Poker takes a lifetime plus one day to master;

(e) "Sh!t happens"!

9. **Take Your Time -** There is no need to rush any aspect of poker whether you are playing, studying or preparing. One of the biggest lessons I have learned about becoming a better player is that patience is an important part of the game and to practice it at every turn. As the saying goes – "all (good) things come to those who wait". Nothing could be more accurate, and by exercising a little patience along with a dose of discipline, your game will go to new heights of enjoyment, thrills and challenges.

10. **Don't Let Poker Rule –** I have a bit of an addictive personality and up until a few years ago my life was never lived in the slow lane. As a result I have had to learn some hard lessons but I have also learned to temper my involvement in the things I love with a bit of balance and moderation. If you find that poker has become all consuming, the bank account is being drained, the family is on the verge of moving out or you are close to losing your job then you must take some big steps to correct the situation. Hopefully you will be able to recognise the symptoms a long time before playing has an adverse effect on your life and do something about it. If not, here is a website worth visiting - www.gamblersanonymous.org

Research Question 16

Where was Joe Hachem born
and where did he grow up?

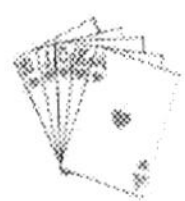

I hope you have enjoyed my book and through reading it either discovered a passion for Poker or enriched one that already existed.

May you enjoy many hours, days weeks and even years of pleasure from this game and the challenges that lay ahead.

Now - crank up the volume on a bit of Kenny Rogers – "The Gambler" or for those who are not quite so old maybe a little Lady Gaga – "Pokerface" or "Deal" by the Grateful Dead. Either way we need to set the scene for our next lot of poker moves.

In closing, in the immortal words of Douglas Noel Adams of "A Hitchhiker's Guide to the Galaxy" fame;

"So long and thanks for all the fish!"

All the best,
Jim.

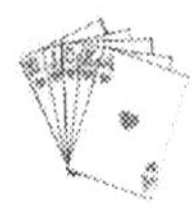

FISH 'N' CHIPS - ANSWER GUIDE

LESSON 3 - HAND EXAMPLES

SINGLE WINNER HANDS

Exercise 1

Player 1 = Straight – 4 to 8
Player 2 = Straight – 9 to J
Player 3 = Straight – 4 to 9
Player 4 = One Pair – J's

Player 2 - has the best hand with the highest straight.

Exercise 2

Player 1 = Three of a kind (Trip) - J's with 8 kicker
Player 2 = Full House - J's over 5's
Player 3 = Two Pair - A's and J's
Player 4 = Straight – 5 to 9

Player 2 – wins with Full House.

Exercise 3

Player 1 = Full House - Q's over K's
Player 2 = Full House - Q's over K's
Player 3 = Full House - Q's over 7's
Player 4 = Full House - Q's over A's

Player 4 – wins as his Full House is made with a bigger pair – Aces.

Exercise 4

Player 1 = High Card – A-K-Q- (7) -5
Player 2 = High Card – A-K-Q- (10) -8
Player 3 = High Card – A-K-Q- (J) -7
Player 4 = High Card – A-K-Q- (9) -7

Player 3 - Each player holds A-K-Q as they are on the board but Player 3 holds the next highest kicker – the Jack.

Exercise 5

Player 1 = Two pair - K's & 8's with J kicker
Player 2 = Two pair - K's & 4's with 8 kicker
Player 3 = Two pair - K's & 4's with A kicker
Player 4 = Two pair - K's & 8's with Q kicker

Player 4 - Highest two pair but beats Player 1 with the highest kicker – the Queen.

Exercise 6

Player 1 = Flush – 10-9- (8) -3-2
Player 2 = Two Pair – 3's and 10's with A kicker
Player 3 = Three of a kind (Trips) - 10's with K kicker
Player 4 = Flush – 10-9- (7) -4-3

Player 1 - Has the highest Flush 10- 9- (8) and beats Player 4's flush 10-9- (7)

Exercise 7

Player 1 = Straight 8 to Q
Player 2 = Three of a kind, (Set)– 10's with A kicker
Player 3 = Straight 10 -A
Player 4 = Two Pair – Q's & 3's

Player 3 - Holds the highest straight 10 - A

Exercise 8

Player 1 = Full house – J's over A's
Player 2 = Full house – Q's over A's
Player 3 = Full house – Q's over J's
Player 4 = Straight – 10 to A

Player 2 - Has the highest full house. (Note: Player 3's third J does not count because the Q makes the higher full house).

Exercise 9

Player 1 = Two pair – J's and 2's
Player 2 = Two pair – J's and 4's
Player 3 = Two pair – J's and 2's
Player 4 = Two pair – K's and 2's

Player 4 - Has the highest two pair with the K's

Exercise 10

Player 1 = Straight - 2 to 6 (Note: Ace does not count)
Player 2 = Flush – A-K- (6) -4-2
Player 3 = Flush – A-K- (7) -4- 2
Player 4 = Flush – A-K- (4) -3-2

Player 3 - Has the highest Flush with the A-K- (7).

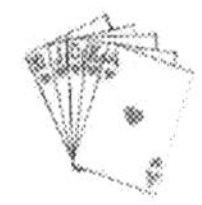

Exercise 11

Player 1 = Four of a kind (Quads) – 8,s
Player 2 = Two pair – 10's & 8's with a A kicker
Player 3 = Straight Flush – 7 to J
Player 4 = Full House – 7's over 8's

Player 3 - Smashes this hand with a Straight Flush.

Exercise 12

Player 1 = Four of a kind – K's with Q kicker
Player 2 = Four of a kind – K's with Q kicker
Player 3 = Four of a kind – K's with Q kicker
Player 4 = Four of a kind – K's with A kicker

Player 4 – Holds the Quads with an A kicker

Exercise 13

Player 1 = Trip – 7's with 10 kicker
Player 2 = Two pair - 7's and 2's
Player 3 = Trip – 7's with K kicker
Player 4 = Two pair - 10's and 8's (Note: 7 counts as a kicker)

Player 3 – Holds the Trips with a K kicker

Exercise 14

Player 1 = Straight - A to 5
Player 2 = Straight - A to 5
Player 3 = Straight - 2 to 6
Player 4 = Straight - A to 5

Player 3 – The board shows a straight A to 5, but Player 3 has the 6 to make the higher straight.

Exercise 15

Player 1 = One Pair – 8's with A kicker
Player 2 = One Pair – 9's
Player 3 = One Pair – 8's with Q kicker
Player 4 = One Pair – 10's

Player 4 – Holds the highest pair – 10's.

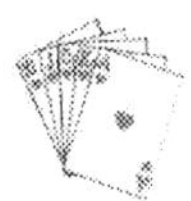

Lesson 3 - Additional exercises

SPLIT POTS

Exercise 1

All Players hold a Straight Flush - 4 to 8. Any player holding the 9 of spades would have won the hand but as the highest hand is on the board, the pot is split four ways.

Exercise 2

Player 1 = Full House - J's over 5's
Player 2 = Full House - J's over 5's
Player 3 = Two pair – A's & J's
Player 4 = Straight - 5 to 9

Players 1 & 2 – Both hold the same Full House hand and so it is a two-way split pot.

Exercise 3

Player 1 = Full House - Q's over K's
Player 2 = Full House - Q's over K's
Player 3 = Full House - Q's over A's
Player 4 = Full House - Q's over A's

Players 3 & 4 – Both hold the same higher Full House hand and the pot is split two ways.

Exercise 4

All players win as they hold the winning hand Ace high with K-Q-J-9 kickers, which is on the board. No player holds higher cards or a pair the pot is split four ways.

Exercise 5

All players win as they hold the winning hand Flush K-J-10-9-8, which is on the board. As no player holds a higher spade than the 8 it is a four-way split pot.

Exercise 6

Player 1 = Straight – 8 to Q
Player 2 = Straight – 7 to J (on the board)
Player 3 = Straight – 7 to J (on the board)
Player 4 = Straight – 8 to Q

Players 1 & 4 – Both hold the Q high straight and therefore the pot is split two ways.

Exercise 7

Player 1 = One Pair – 3's with A, K, Q kickers
Player 2 = High Card – Ace with K, Q, 10, 5 kickers
Player 3 = One Pair – 3's, with A, K, Q kickers
Player 4 = One Pair – 3's, with A, K, Q kickers

Players 1, 3 & 4 – Each hold a pair of 3's and therefore the pot is split three ways.

Exercise 8

Player 1 = Full house – A's over J's
Player 2 = Full house – A's over J's
Player 3 = Full house – A's over J's
Player 4 = Straight – 10 to A

Players 1, 2 & 3 – Each hold the same Full House and therefore the pot is split three ways.

Exercise 9

Player 1 = Three of a kind – J's
Player 2 = Straight – 2 to 6 (Note:- The Ace does not count)
Player 3 = Straight – 2 to 6
Player 4 = One Pair – K's

Players 2 & 3 – Each hold the same hand and therefore the pot is split two ways.

Exercise 10

Player 1 = Two pair – A's & K's with Q kicker.
Player 2 = Two pair – A's & K's with 6 kicker.
Player 3 = Two pair – A's & K's with 9 kicker.
Player 4 = Two pair – A's & K's with Q kicker.

Players 1 & 4 – Both hold the same Two Pair with a Q kicker hand and so it is a two-way split pot. (Note:- Player 4's Pair of Queens do not count as only one is used as the kicker).

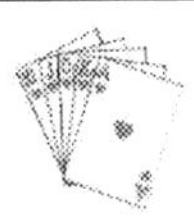

LESSON 5 - REVIEW ANSWERS

Element 1: Multiple Choices Quiz

1 – (C)	2 – (C)	3 – (A)	4 – (B)
5 – (D)	6 – (B)	7 – (D)	8 – (D)
9 – (C)	10 – (D)	11 – (B)	12 – (C)

Element 2: Short Answer Questions

1. Don't annoy the bad players because they may leave taking potential winnings with them.

2. Luck is part of the game however working and learning the game will reduce your dependability on luck.

3. Cards that are on the board that a greater in value than those you hold.

4. When it appears on the board.

5. King and Queen.

6. No.

7. Never, the big blind is always posted.

8. Normally half.

9. Yes, but they are not allowed to comment.

10. When the cards become marked in any way.

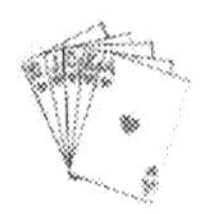

Element 3 : Crossword

Solution:

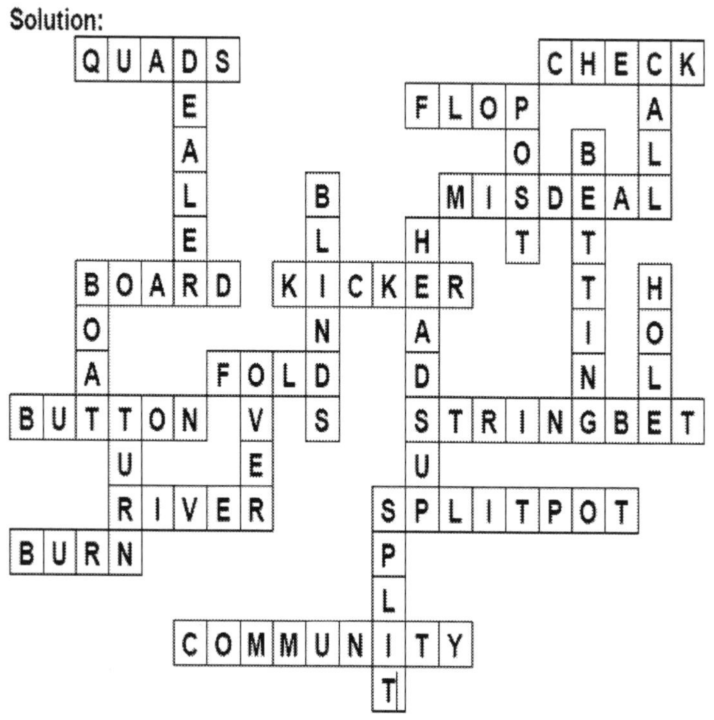

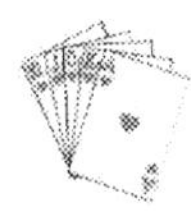

Lesson 10 - A Little More Review

Element 1: Multiple Choices Quiz

1 – (C)	2 – (B)	3 – (D)	4 – (D)	5 – (A)
6 – (C)	7 – (C)	8 – (C)	9 – (D)	10 – (C)
11 – (D)	12 – (C)	13 – (D)	14 – (D)	15 - (C)

Element 2: Short Answer Questions

1. Table position, stack size, cards you hold.
2. Players, chips and cards.
3. Perseverance, Education and Association.
4. Doyle Brunson won the world series of poker twice with this hand.
5. Use and comply with a bankroll requirements.
6. Specific relevant and timely.
7. Continue to play using play money, while focussing on the "PEA".
8. Peer and self-assessment.
9. Finding a coach or mentor.
10. That's how we find out who we are.

Element 3: True or False

1 – True	2 – False	3 – True	4 – False
5 – False	6 – True	7 – True	8 –True
9 – True	10 – False	11 – True	12 - False

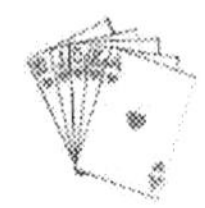

Lesson 11 – Learning Our Language

Element 2: Crossword Challenge A - J

Solution:

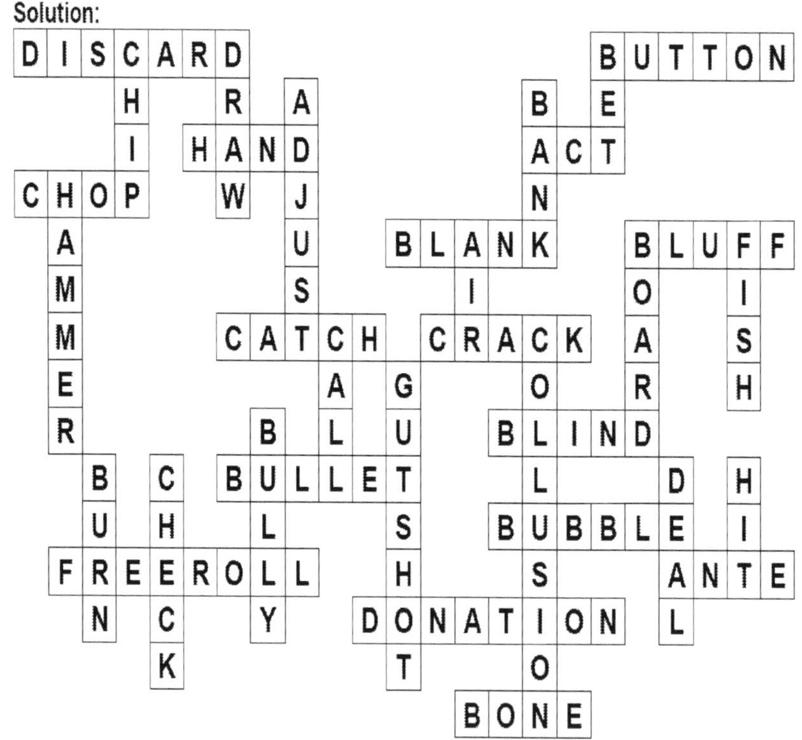

Element 4: Crossword Challenge K - Z

Solution:

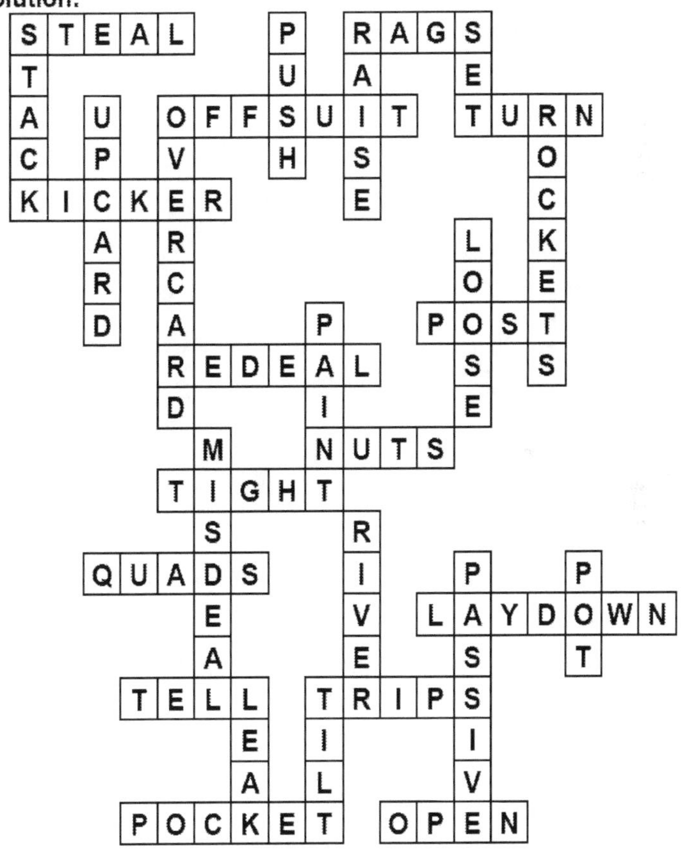

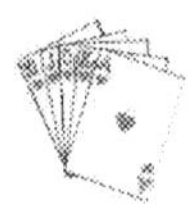

ANSWERS TO RESEARCH QUESTIONS

1. As at January 2012, Phil Hellmuth with 11, all of which are for Texas Hold'em.

2. Stu Ungar, Johnny Moss.

3. To have something to smell if players start smoking.

4. Jesus.

5. The King of Spades is said to represent David, King of Israel; the King of Clubs - Alexander the Great; the King of Hearts - the French King Charlemagne; and the King of Diamonds is said to represent the Roman Caesar, Augustus.

6. Chris has been clocked throwing a card at 71 mph and has cut through things from bananas to melons.

7. Mike Caro is "the Mad Genius"; Paul Magriel is "X-22"; Howard Lederer is "the Professor" and Robert Williamson is "Mr. Omaha".

8. Zero in cash and personal debts to multiple players.

9. He was a professional magician before he became a poker player.

10. Two – the Jack of Heart and the Jack of Spades

11. 5 or 10.

12. Phil Ivey - a Flush

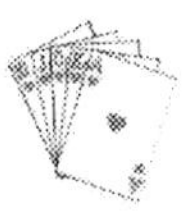

13. 1970 - Johnny Moss.

14. 424 to 1.

15. Kid Poker.

16. Joe Hachem was born in Lebanon, and grew up in Australia.

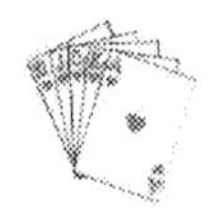

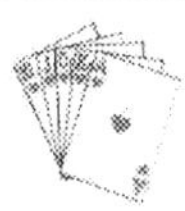

ACKNOWLEDGEMENTS

I would like to thank you for buying this book as well as all the other poker players who have entertained, advised, astounded and inspired through television, the web and books. Without this community the journey would be pointless and the production of this book impossible.

I would also like to thank Ken, my friend to whom this book is dedicated. His editorial contribution and advice have been invaluable.

Finally I would like to thank my wife Vicky, whose tireless efforts wading through the pages ensuring my spelling, grammar and layout were spot on. If not for her support and dedication this project would not have been realised.